Charles C Ayer

The Tragic Heroines of Pierre Corneille

A study in French literature of the seventeenth century

Charles C Ayer

The Tragic Heroines of Pierre Corneille
A study in French literature of the seventeenth century

ISBN/EAN: 9783337213862

Printed in Europe, USA, Canada, Australia, Japan

Cover: Foto ©ninafisch / pixelio.de

More available books at **www.hansebooks.com**

THE TRAGIC HEROINES

OF

PIERRE CORNEILLE

A STUDY IN FRENCH LITERATURE OF THE
SEVENTEENTH-CENTURY.

A DISSERTATION

PRESENTED TO THE

PHILOSOPHICAL FACULTY OF THE UNIVERSITY
OF STRASSBURG

FOR THE PURPOSE OF OBTAINING THE DEGREE
OF DOCTOR OF PHILOSOPHY

BY

CHARLES CARLTON AYER

STRASSBURG
PRINTED BY J. H. ED. HEITZ (HEITZ & MÜNDEL)
1898.

The subject of the following pages was suggested to the writer by Professor Gröber of the University of Strassburg. The writer takes this opportunity of thanking Professor Gröber for his kind assistance and encouragement during the progress of the work, as well as for the many valuable hours passed under his instruction.

CONTENTS.

Theories in regard to his...
...cratic birth ....
...ate number ....
...pe ....

..., which gradually became a...
... system.

...re» ....
...ic element ....
...sol and power of dissu...
...reeding ....
...rit ....
...d charms and attributes
....

INTRODUCTION

The object of the present essay is to call back from oblivion the heroines of the great Corneille; for it is not too much to say that the vast majority of them have long since passed out of the recollection and interest of the public. Even in France, the land of their birth, they are with few exceptions forgotten. It is only with difficulty that one recalls the names of some half a dozen of the best known among them.[1] This fact surprises us, when we reflect that in the seventeenth century, Corneille was venerated as the father of French tragedy, and that the birth of each new daughter was a literary event of no small importance. For nearly forty years, from the production of his first tragedy, MÉDÉE, in 1635 down to 1672. when he closed his literary career with SURÉNA, Corneille dominated the French stage. To be sure, his popularity toward the last was not as great as it was in the days of his early masterpieces. The peculiar genius of Racine had gradually won the public over to a new style of tragedy, where love and not the heroic conflict of duty and passion, was the theme. But the

---

[1] Even Guizot (Corneille et son temps, p. 256, Paris 1813) makes the blunder of calling the heroine of PERTHARITE Rosamunde instead of Rodelinde, and in a second revised edition of 1852, this error remains uncorrected. The heroine is called by her right name, however, on p. 222.

reputation of Corneille still remained great to the end, as is attested by Mme. de Sévigné in many a letter subsequent to the year 1669, when many critics would have us believe that the star of Corneille had long since set.

It does not take long to mention the heroines of Corneille whose names are familiar to the general reading public. Everybody knows and admires Chimène, the heroine of the CID, as one of the most unique creations in the whole realm of tragedy. The famous curse of Camille still makes the heroine of HORACE a favorite with ambitious young debutantes. The Émilie of CINNA is known as the most typical of Corneille's «adorable furies»; and the Pauline of POLYEUCTE stands alone as the proof that Corneille could create a tender womanly heroine, if he chose to do so. These four heroines are generally known, because they are the leading female figures in the four masterpieces of Corneille, and as such are discussed in the numerous histories of French literature. But these heroines of four tragedies form but a small minority in the total number; for Corneille, it should be remembered, was the author of twenty-four tragedies or heroic dramas.

Only the special student of Corneille now-a-days is at all interested in the remainder of the poet's female characters; in the fact, for example, that Médée with her tragic cry of «Moi!»[1] struck the key note of the Corneille heroine; that Théodore failed to please, because a heroine threatened with the ignominy of prostitution was shocking to the French ideas of propriety; that Rodogune was the heroine of the play which Corneille regarded as his best work; that the Cléopatre in the same play furnished Lessing with material for one of his bitterest attacks on the classic French tragedy;[2] that Rodelinde, who was regarded as largely responsible for the failure of

---

[1] MÉDÉE, 1. V 320.
[2] Hamburger Dramaturgie No. 29.

PERTHARITE served later as the inspiration to Racine's ANDROMAQUE; that Dircé, Viriate and Éryxe were special favorites of Corneille, because, as he said, they were purely the products of his own powers of invention;[1] that the Bérénice who brought Corneille into direct competition with his younger rival, Racine, was no other than Henriette d'Angleterre, subduing her passion for Louis XIV; that Pulchérie aroused great expectations in Mme. de Sévigné,[2] only to meet with a cool reception from the Parisian public;[3] and finally, that Corneille's last heroine, Eurydice, died with a cry on her lips worthy of the most sublime tragic heroine.

These casual comments on the unknown and forgotten heroines of Corneille, show us that in their day they were regarded as personages of importance. Why then have they passed so completely into oblivion?

It is the custom of most writers on French literature in treating of Corneille, to say that his greatest period of popularity lasted from 1636, when his tragic genius burst forth in all its power in LE CID, to 1652, when the utter failure of PERTHARITE drove him into temporary retirement; further, that on his return to the theatre in 1659, he found the public taste changed, the love tragedies of Quinault having in the meantime supplanted his own heroic dramas in public favor. Hence the gradual decadence of his fame down to the end of his career, notwithstanding many admirable points in all of his later plays.

It is also the custom to dismiss briefly even those plays which belong to the first period. The four masterpieces are the only ones which receive adequate treatment, and it is precisely in limiting ourselves to these four plays, that we fail to arrive

---

[1] Examen d'ŒDIPE; SERTORIUS, Au Lecteur; and SOPHONISBE, Au Lecteur.
[2] Lettre du 15 Janvier 1672. Mme. de Sévigné à Mme. de Grignan.
[3] Lettre du 24 Février 1673. Mme. de Coulanges à Mme. de Sévigné.

at a true estimate of Corneille's real worth as a dramatist. Likewise in considering critically only Chimène, Camille, Émilie, and Pauline, we do not begin to get at a real understanding of the poet's own point of view in regard to his heroines.

As far as we know, no comparative study of these heroines has as yet been undertaken. In looking over the mass of literature on Corneille,[1] we find only isolated statements concerning a few individual heroines, or general criticisms praising or condemning them, according to the writer and his mood. Some of the opinions of Corneille's contemporaries are worth noting; for instance, the abusive criticism showered upon Chimène by Scudéry[2] and the Académie;[3] the declaration of Balzac that no writer of antiquity had ever produced heroines to be compared with Émilie and Sabine;[4] the proposal of the Abbé d'Aubignac[5] to alter the climax of HORACE by making Camille throw herself upon the sword of her brother, instead of being pursued to her death by him; the opinion of St. Évremond[6] on Corneille's masterly delineation of the characters of Cornélie and Sophonisbe; the antipathy which Racine[7] expresses for women who are more masculine than the heroes to whom they give their lessons in heroism; the defence by Corneille[8] of the heroic type and his disapproval of the tender type adopted by Quinault and brought to perfection by Racine.

These isolated bits of criticism are interesting, but they belong to a period long since past. They possess no living interest. They furnish us with no clew by which we can explain

[1] E. Picot. Bibliographie Cornélienne, Paris 1876.
[2] Observations sur le CID, Paris 1637.
[3] Les sentiments de l'Académie Française sur la tragi-comédie du Cid Paris 1638.
[4] Lettre à Corneille 17 Jan. 1643.
[5] La Pratique du Théâtre 1657, p. 82.
[6] SOPHONISBE, Au Lecteur.
[7] Dissertation sur l'ALEXANDRE de Racine, Oeuvres choisies, p. 167, edition Firmin Didot, Paris 1852.
[8] Première Préface de BRITANNICUS 1667.

to ourselves the general indifference that prevails to-day in regard to Corneille's heroines. It is for this reason that we make them the object of a special study, which shall, as far as possible, make clear the poet's ideas on the subject. By comparing them with one another, we may perhaps see why they have not held their place on the stage.

But before we begin the examination of the tragedies, in which our heroines appear, it is first necessary to have clearly in mind the general character of the life, manners, and literature of the seventeenth century in France. Two facts impress themselves at once upon us; first, the literature of the age was entirely under aristocratic influence; and secondly, the *chefs d'œuvre* of this golden age of French literature were masterpieces written according to rules. Perhaps these two facts may not be without their bearing on the heroines of Corneille.

The influence of polite society [1] on the literature of the seventeenth century in France, is not to be under estimated, and specially the influence of the ladies, those *grandes dames*, whose names add such lustre to the century of Louis XIV.

In no department of literature was their interest more keen than in the drama. This is to be explained by the fact that up to the year 1618, no lady could with decency go to the theatre, and that the elevation of the stage to a plane of respectability had just been accomplished, when the Marquise de Rambouillet opened her famous salon.[2] In 1620 the Hôtel Rambouillet came into existence, and began at once to exert its refining influence on all who came within its precincts. The object of the mistress of the Blue Chamber was not to estab-

---

[1] Victor Cousin. La Société Française an XVII° siècle d'après le «GRAND CYRUS» de Mlle. de Scudéry. Paris 1858. 4th edition, 2 vol. Paris 1873.

[2] Breitinger. Der Salon Rambouillet und seine kulturhistorische Bedeutung, Zürich 1874.

lish a literary tribunal. Her idea was simply to form a fashionable and agreeable rendez-vous for high society where literary people could meet the members of the cultivated nobility in social intercourse. All serious literary work she gladly left to be attended to at the Saturday receptions of Mlle. de Scudéry.[1] Mme. de Rambouillet was not a writer, though she was a distinguished patron of letters; she was not a politician, even if some of the ladies who mingled in her salon, did allow themselves to become involved in political schemes; and she was not a prude, if she did make it her object to keep out of her house the tone of licentiousness which had disgraced the court of Henri IV, and to cultivate within her walls the true ideals of hospitality, honor and politeness.

The influence of the Hôtel Rambouillet lasted unimpaired from 1620 to 1645, when the marriage and departure of the beautiful Julie d'Angennes, daughter of the Marquise de Rambouillet announced that the famous salon was nearing its end. The final dissolution was caused in 1648 by the death of Voiture, one of the most elegant conversationists of the Blue Chamber, and by the termination of the war of the Fronde, which dispersed many of the most important members of that brilliant society.

The fame and influence of the Hôtel Rambouillet were, therefore, at their height during those years, when Corneille was engaged in producing his greatest and most enduring masterpieces. During his frequent visits to Paris he was always a welcome guest at the Wednesday receptions. He had the honor of reading POLYEUCTE before the Marquise and the chagrin of hearing afterwards that his religious tragedy had not pleased her. But he also had the satisfaction of knowing that his tragedies in general and especially his tragic heroines, found

---

[1] Rathéry et Boutrou. Mlle. de Scudéry, sa vie et sa correspondance avec un choix de ses poésies. Paris 1873.

great favor in the eyes of certain ladies of Mme. de Rambouillet's coterie. The Hôtel Rambouillet had a great influence on Corneille, as we shall see.

The second of the elements which is inseparably asssociated with the seventeenth century in France, is the preponderance of rules in all departments of literature. As time went on, individuality of creation was more and more discouraged, and those writers were regarded as the greatest geniuses, who produced works in closest accordance with the rules. To defy the rules was not only to subject one's self to merciless ridicule, but to place one's self beyond the pale of serious consideration. To please according to the rules was the end and aim of every judicious writer.

Malherbe[1] is the first great literary law-giver of the seventeenth century. His field was poetry. The rules which he laid down were recognized by Boileau, and accepted as infallible by future poets for the next two centuries. Corneille profited by many of his suggestions. Malherbe forbade all rhyme which appealed only to the ear (apparent, conquérant); rhyme between a simple and a compound word (temps, printemps); or between words of similar nature (père, mère); or between proper names (Lysandre, Alexandre); or between a long and a short syllable (âme, dictame); or a rhyme between the middle of a line and the end. Hiatus and *enjambement* were likewise strictly forbidden.

Balzac[2] with the same discrimination established the rules of prose. Just as Malherbe made it his life work to free the French poetry from Greek, Latin, and *patois* elements, so

---

[1] Oeuvres de Messire François de Malherbe, Gentilhomme ordinaire de la Chambre du Roy 1630. See Blanchemain edition, Paris 1877. See also Gournay. Malherbe, sa vie et ses oeuvres, Paris 1852.

[2] Oeuvres. 2 vol. Paris 1665. Edition Conrart; Edition Malitourne 1822, 2 vol. Edition Moreau Paris 1854, 2 vol. Lettres inédites de Balzac, Tamizey de Larroque, Paris 1872.

Balzac resolved to fix the rules of a prose style which should be purely and nationally French and not the French of a Rabelais, Amyot or Montaigne, or indeed of any author however gifted, who might hitherto have written. A glance at the LETTRES and ENTRETIENS of Balzac shows us at once his theories as to the use of hyperbole, the periodic construction of sentences, the skillful use of antitheses and metaphors. Corneille also made use of many of these points and delighted especially in antitheses and symmetry of construction.

In 1635, the Académie Française [1] was founded. The primary object of this body was simply to establish the rules of the French language, and on these lines the plans of a grammar were drawn up by Chapelain, and the compilation of the DICTIONNAIRE DE L'ACADÉMIE FRANCAISE was entrusted to Vaugelas. But soon after the establishment of the institution, an event occurred, which changed for the moment the policy of the academicians. This event was the production of LE CID in 1636. Through the jealousy of Scudéry and Richlieu. the question as to the faults and merits of the new work was brought before the Académie. As we now contemplate the immortal fame which this masterpiece of French tragedy enjoys, it matters but little to us that the Académie taking sides with Scudéry, declared that the new play was contrary to the rules. The one point which arrests our attention is that the word «règles» was thereby introduced into dramatic criticism with an intensity and a significance hitherto unknown. The Académie criticised Corneille for the subject matter of the CID, and for his manner of dealing with it. They also disapproved of the character of the heroine. But the greatest objection

---

[1] Pellisson et Abbé d'Olivet. Histoire de l'Académie, 2 vol. Paris 1729. (1635-1652 by Pellisson, 1652-1700 by d'Olivet) new edition by Ch. Livet, Paris 1858, 2 vol.

P. Mesnard. Histoire politique de l'Académie Française, Paris 1858.

which was raised was that Corneille had violated the law of the unities.

The law of the three unities of time, place and action is popularly regarded as the characteristic *par excellence* of the classic French tragedy, almost indeed, as the special invention of the classic French dramatists according to the teachings of Aristotle. But this is not so. In France the law of the three unities was construed into a national dramatic dogma by Chapelain in 1637, as a result of the quarrel over the CID. But if we examine the literature of other nations previous to the CID we shall find that the unities were known, even if they were not strictly observed in the other European countries long before the time of Corneille[1] by such writers as Trissino[2] in Italy, Sir Philip Sidney[3] and Ben Jonson[4] in England, by Cervantes[5] and Tirso de Molina[6] in Spain. Lope de Vega[7] even makes a protest against being hampered by what he regards as a needless hindrance to the dramatist.

In France, as we have said, the law of the unities found favor, because it was a law. It increased the difficulty to be surmounted. It was one of those very strains on the dramatist's powers of invention in which Corneille of all poets gloried. The CID was a masterpiece, but was against the rules. Corneille, therefore, deferred to the opinions of the Académie, and yielding to the pressure in the literary atmosphere about him, he never again presumed nor desired to assert his independence of the rules. On the contrary, beginning with HORACE, he

---

[1] Breitinger. Les unités d'Aristote avant le Cid de Corneille, Genève 1879.

[2] La Poetica. Divisioni quattro. Vicenza 1529; in edition of 1563, supplementary chapters on comedy and tragedy.

[3] An Apologie for Poetrie 1595. See Arbor's English reprints, Lond. 1868.

[4] Prologue to every Man in his Humour 1598.

[5] Don Quijote 1610. I 48.

[6] Los Cigarrales de Toledo Madrid 1624.

[7] Rima con el arte nuevo de hacer comedias. 1609. obras sueltas IV.

adhered closely to them, and remained to the end of his career, a classicist in the strictest French acceptance of the term.

What were then the special characteristics of the classic French tragedy? What were the other rules besides the law of the unities?

In order to understand the requisites of the classic school, as distinguished from the romantic school, we must examine the works of a great number of tragic dramatists. It is not sufficient to begin with Corneille as inventor of the classic school. His title of father of the French tragedy is contestable, for he owed much, especially in the matter of minor details to his literary ancestors and contemporaries. We must be familiar with Jodelle,[1] Garnier,[2] Montchrestien,[3] Mairet[4] and many other lesser dramatists, before we can appreciate the perfection of outer form attained by Corneille. Many persons rate Racine above Corneille, but Racine and after him, Voltaire could not but have acknowledged that they owed an immeasurable debt of gratitude to Corneille for establishing for them and in behalf of the literary glory of France the canons of the national tragedy.

Briefly stated, the classicists of the French school were idealists and maintained that tragedy should represent only the noble and dignified in art to the exclusion of the grotesque or comic; that reason should be the poet's guide and not his own unbridled fancies or poetical caprices; that the true models and subjects were to be found in antiquity in the history and mythology of ancient Greece and Rome, and not in contemporaneous subjects of modern times and nations; that the classic tragedy must have a fixed form, a fixed number of acts

---

[1] 1532-1573.
[2] 1545-1601.
[3] 1575-1621.
[4] 1604-1686.

and lines without *enjambement* and with regular caesura and appropriate rhyme, in short, the monotonous, though exquisitely perfect system of versification of Malherbe and Boileau ; that the action, the actual bodily exertion of the actors be reduced to a minimum, that no scene of violence, except suicide, be enacted on the open stage, and that its place be supplied by narrations to confidants, or by stately monologues which should apprise the spectator of the course of events without detracting from the dignified deportment of the personages ; and finally, that the play must conform to the law of the three unities of time, place and action, mentioned above, and most happily formulated in the well known couplet of Boileau,

> Qu'en un lieu, en un jour, un seul fait accompli
> Tienne jusqu'à la fin le théâtre rempli.[1]

The history of the maintenance of the «règles» down to the rise of the romantic school in the nineteenth century would form a whole chapter in itself. For our present purpose, however, it suffices to say that the rules which governed the masterpieces of Corneille, were perpetuated by Racine and Voltaire and justified themselves, at least from the French point of view, by the production of tragedies which hold a permanent place in the *répertoire* of the Théâtre Français. It is the custom to exalt Racine at the expense of Voltaire, but no one can deny that in ZAIRE and MÉROPE, Voltaire produced two plays that entitle him to rank with the first dramatists of the French stage. Toward the close of seventeenth century occurred the famous quarrel of the Ancients and the Moderns. Perrault[2] maintained in an excess of national enthusiasm that the authors of the France of the seventeenth century totally eclipsed the

---
[1] Art poétique 45-46.
[2] Parallèle des Anciens et des Modernes 1688-1693, 2 vol.

great writers of antiquity, that Malherbe was superior to Horace, Molière to Plautus, La Fontaine to Phaedrus. Boileau [1] the foremost critic of the century, did not share the views of Perrault, but he did express it as his opinion that antiquity had produced no tragedies, which could be compared with the classic masterpieces of the century of Louis XIV.

Corneille died in 1684, Racine in 1699, leaving the national faith in the rules unshaken. In the eighteenth century, Voltaire with his learning, his talent, and above all, with his revolutionary nature, might easily, by the sheer force of his own individuality, have overturned the dramatic tenets of the previous century. As it was, in his natural restlessness, he introduced certain innovations, which had not characterized the works of his predecessors. He extended the field of psychological possibilities. Whereas Corneille had always dwelt on the conflict between duty and passion, and Racine on love, as the only mainsprings of tragic action, Voltaire studied paternal or family love in ZULIME, BRUTUS, SÉMIRAMIS, MÉROPE, L'ORPHELIN DE LA CHINE; the sentiment of christianity in ZAIRE and ALZIRE; the sentiment of chivalry in TANCRÈDE. He also made his plays more interesting by strengthening the action and hastening the movement, and by varying the scene of action, which Corneille and Racine had always had a predilection for placing in Greece, Rome, or tributary provinces. Voltaire laid the scene of his dramas in Palestine (MARIANNE, ZAIRE), in South America (ALZIRE), in Sicily (TANCRÈDE), and in China (L'ORPHELIN DE LA CHINE). He also deftly managed to weave his philosophical views into his plays, in order that he might instruct as well as amuse. Voltaire's services to the French tragedy were, therefore, considerable; but he nevertheless remained classic at heart and cast his plays in that classic mould, which he had been brought up to reverence.

---

[1] Lettre à M. Perrault, 1700.

His devotion to the cause of the classic tragedy is also to be attributed in a large measure to his confidence in the good taste of his nation in all matters whether literary or otherwise. The expression «bon gout» is a favorite one with Voltaire, whenever he wishes to praise his own people at the expense of other nations. It was no invention of his, however; Mme. de Sévigné[1] had previously used it in one of her effusions on Corneille.

In 1719 Voltaire produced his first tragedy, OEDIPE, which met with the conventional favor. From 1726 to 1729, political events caused him to abide in England. During this sojourn, he became acquainted with the works of a dramatic poet, whose name and fame had hardly yet crossed the channel. This man was Shakespeare.[2] With his keen insight, Voltaire recognized at once the transcendent genius of the British poet, but he deplored the fact that such a genius should be so ignorant or negligent of dramatic rules.[3] Voltaire was not alone in his opinion; for at this time, England herself stood under the spell of the French classic school, and the CATO of Addison, produced in 1713, and written according to French models, was considered the finest tragedy on the English stage. Voltaire borrowd but little from Shakespeare. From OTHELLO he conceived the idea of basing his tragedy of ZAIRE on the passion of jealousy. But in all other respects, he remained as classic as before. In his tragedy of TANCRÈDE in 1761 and, in every line of his commentaries on Corneille, published in 1764, we find Voltaire a firm adherent to the doctrine of the classic tragedy founded on rules.

Voltaire and his followers, Marmontel,[4] Laharpe[5] and Le-

---

[1] Lettre du 16 Mars 1672.
[2] See J. J. Jusserand. Shakespeare en France sous l'Ancien Régime. Cosmopolis, Nov. 1896.
[3] Dissertation sur la Tragédie; Seconde Lettre à M. Falkener.
[4] Éléments de littérature, 1787.
[5] Lycée ou Cours de littérature ancienne et moderne, 16 vol. Paris 1799-1805.

mercier¹ testify to the force, which the rules possessed in France throughout the eighteenth century and down to the rise of the romantic school. Nevertheless opponents to classicism were not entirely wanting. Diderot made a plea for the introduction of a *bourgeois* element in tragedy, maintaining as Corneille had maintained long years before that there was no good and sufficient reason, why kings and queens should monopolize the tragic stage. The standpoint of Diderot is precisely that of Lessing, the difference between the two men being in this respect that Diderot with all his theories did not succeed in producing a work which should make his standpoint convincing,² while Lessing produced a masterpiece in his EMILIA GALOTTI, a tragedy with a *bourgeois* heroine.

One other name, that of Mercier, is worthy of mention in the eighteenth century, not because he had the eccentricity to declare his own works superior to those of Corneille and Racine, but because he came boldly forward with the courage of his convictions and denounced the fundamental principle of the French classic drama, the theory of a hard and fast dramatic system. In the present connection it is interesting to note his opinion that the rules «mutilated the characters».³ Could he have had the heroines of Corneille in mind when he made this statement? We shall see.

In any case the heroines of Corneille must have been created under peculiar circumstances. If we assume that a tragedy must conform to certain fixed rules, then we cannot but see that each component part must sustain its certain fixed relation in the general mechanism. And the heroines of Corneille were surely an important element in the poet's dramas.

---

[1] Cours analytique de la littérature 1827.
[2] See his dramas LE FILS NATUREL 1756, and LE PÈRE DE FAMILLE 1758.
[3] See Laharpe vol. V. De Shakespeare.

With the death of Corneille, it is quite natural that the immediate interest in his heroines should have ceased. Other matters soon claimed the attention of the literary public, which was formerly bestowed on them. Thus it is that in the numerous standard histories of French literature, which have appeared in the present century, they are dismissed briefly with a few words of general comment. It is hardly worth while to dwell at length on the conventional opinions expressed by the many writers on French literature. The vast majority agree with the very rational opinions expressed by Voltaire in his COMMENTAIRES SUR CORNEILLE, the most important piece of critical work of the eighteenth century, bearing upon the French tragedy. Voltaire's criticisms are well founded. He objects to the political character of some heroines,[1] to the fondness for argument on the part of others,[2] to the prudishness and insipidity of certain other heroic women at unexpected moments.[3] At the same time he recognizes and admires in them the noble, lofty type of character which makes them distinctively «cornélienne». And in this he is followed by Laharpe,[4] Nisard,[5] Géruzez[6] and Albert.[7] Of late years literary criticism has taken on an analytical aspect. Instead of being moved to pathetic admiration for the generosity, magnanimity, sublimity of the Corneille heroine, we find Hémon[8] calling our attention to the fact that the women of Corneille one and all dwell upon their «gloire» to a degree bordering on monotony,

---

[1] Remarques sur SERTORIUS.
[2] Remarques sur ŒDIPE.
[3] Remarques sur RODOGUNE.
[4] Lycée ou Cours de littérature ancienne et moderne 1799-1805 vol. 5.
[5] Nisard. Histoire de la littérature française ; Paris, 4 vol. 1844-1849, vol. II. ch. 3.
[6] Géruzez, Histoire de la littérature française depuis ses origines jusqu'à la Révolution, Paris 1861, vol. II, p. 94.
[7] Albert. La Littérature française au XVIIe siècle, Paris 1873, p. 94.
[8] Hémon. Théâtre de Pierre Corneille, avec des études sur toutes les tragédies et les comédies. Paris 1886-1887, 4 vol.

and Kreyssig [1] makes the curious observation that the beautiful eyes of Émilie drive Cinna to seek the life of Augustus, while the «*beaux yeux*» of Hermione in Racine's ANDROMAQUE some twenty years later exert the same influence on Oreste and spur him on to a similar deed of daring. These bits of criticism lead us involuntarily to reflect once more on the opinion expressed on Corneille years ago by Sainte Beuve, «His heroines, his adorable furies, are nearly all alike».[2] Perhaps they are. Why should they not be? Corneille worked according to fixed rules. In his long career he must have gradually arrived at a pretty definite conception as to the appropriate functions of a tragic heroine. As he nowhere speaks at length on the subject of heroines, we are obliged to gather and cast into form the stray remarks, which he lets fall here and there, and to prove his theories by direct comparison with the plays themselves. The remarks of Corneille himself in his DISCOURS, AVERTISSEMENTS and EXAMENS will, therefore, form the basis of the first part of this essay. The second part will consist in the enumeration of those details in the delineation of his female characters, which he would seem to have used without knowing it, as unconscious requisites, and in the application of which he was guided by his own innate feelings of propriety and good taste. By thus making the neglected heroines of the great Corneille the subject of a special study, we shall hope, even if we do not succeed in awakening new interest in them, to explain the causes which led to their decline in the seventeenth century and to their complete oblivion in the literary world of to-day.

For purpose of reference we give a list of the female characters of Corneille, showing his method of distributing

---

[1] Kreyssig. Geschichte der französischen Nationallitteratur. Sechste Auflage, vol. 2, p. 30, Berlin 1889.
[2] Sainte-Beuve. Portraits littéraires I p. 47, Paris 1832-1839, 5 vol.

them, together with the number of male characters in each piece.

Médée 1635
  Medée, femme de Jason   2 noble ladies
  Nérine, suivante de Médée   2 confidants
  Créuse, fille de Créon   5 male characters
  Cléone, gouvernante de Créuse

Le Cid 1636
  Dona Urraque, infante de Castille   2 noble ladies
  Léonor, gouvernante de l'Infante   2 confidants
  Chimène, fille de Don Gomez   8 male characters
  Elvire, gouvernante de Chimène

Horace 1640
  Sabine, femme d'Horace et soeur de Curiace   2 noble ladies
  Camille, amante de Curiace et femme d'Horace   1 confidant
  Julie, dame romaine, confidente de Sabine et de Camille   7 male characters

Cinna 1640
  Emilie, fille de C. Joranius, tuteur d'Auguste et proscrit par lui durant le triumvirat   2 noble ladies
  Fulvie, confidente d'Emilie   1 confidant
  Livie, impératrice   6 male characters

Polyeucte 1640
  Pauline, fille de Félix et femme de Polyeucte   1 noble lady
  Stratonice, confidente de Pauline   1 confidant
     7 male characters

Pompée 1641
  Cornélie, femme de Pompée   2 noble ladies
  Cléopatre, soeur de Ptolomée   1 confidant
  Charmion, dame d'honneur de Cléopatre   8 male characters

Rodogune 1644
    Cléopatre, reine de Syrie, veuve de Demetrius Nicanor   2 noble ladies
    Laonice, confidente de Cléopatre   1 confidant
    Rodogune, soeur de Phraates, roi des Parthes   4 male characters

Théodore 1645
    Théodore, princesse d'Antioche   2 noble ladies
    Marcelle, femme de Valens   1 confidant
    Stéphanie, confidente de Marcelle   6 male characters

Héraclius 1647
    Pulchérie, fille de l'empereur Maurice maîtresse de Martian   3 noble ladies
    Léontine, dame de Constantinople   7 male characters
    Eudoxe, fille de Léontine et maîtresse d'Héraclius

Andromède 1650
    Cassiope, reine d'Éthiopie   2 noble ladies
    Andromède, fille de Céphée et de Cassiope   3 confidants
    Aglante \
    Céphalie } nymphes d'Andromède   5 male characters
    Liriope /

Don Sanche d'Aragon 1650
    D. Isabelle, reine de Castille   3 noble ladies
    Blanche, dame d'honneur de la reine de Castille   1 confidant
    D. Léonor, reine d'Aragon   5 male characters
    D. Elvire, princesse d'Aragon

Nicomède 1651
    Arsinoe, seconde femme de Prusias   2 noble ladies
    Cléone, confidente d'Arsinoe   1 confidant
    Laodice reine d'Arménie   5 male characters

Pertharite 1652
    Rodelinde, femme de Pertharite   2 noble ladies
    Eduïge, soeur de Pertharite   4 male characters

Oedipe 1659
    Jocaste, reine de Thèbes, femme et mère d'Oedipe   2 noble ladies
    Nérine, dame d'honneur   1 confidant
    Dircé, princesse de Thèbes, fille de Laius et de Jocaste, soeur d'Oedipe et amante de Thésée   6 male characters

La Toison d'Or 1660
    Chalciope, fille d'Aete, veuve de Phryxus   3 noble ladies
    Médée, fille d'Aete, amante de Jason   9 male characters
    Hypsipyle, reine de Lemnos

Sertorius 1662
    Aristie, femme de Pompée   2 noble ladies
    Viriate, reine de Lusitanie, à présent Portugal   1 confidant
    Thamire, dame d'honneur de Viriate   6 male characters

Sophonisbe 1663
    Sophonisbe, fille d'Asdrubal, général des Carthaginois, et reine de Numidie   2 noble ladies
    Herminie, dame d'honneur de Sophonisbe   2 confidants
    Éryxe, reine de Gétulie   7 male characters
    Barcée, dame d'honneur d'Éryxe

Othon 1664
    Camille nièce de Galba   2 noble ladies
    Albiane, soeur d'Albin et dame d'honneur de Camille   2 confidants
    Plautine, fille de Vinius, amante d'Othon   8 male characters
    Flavie, amie de Plautine

Agésilas 1666
   Mandane, soeur de Spitridate   3 noble ladies
   Elpinice ⎫
             ⎬ filles de Lysandre   6 male characters
   Aglatide ⎭

Attila 1667
   Honorie, soeur de l'empéreur Valentin   2 noble ladies
   Flavie, dame d'honneur d'Honorie   1 confidant
   Ildione, soeur de Mérovée, roi de France   4 male characters

Tite et Bérénice 1670
   Bérénice, reine d'une partie de Judée   2 noble ladies
   Domitie, fille de Corbulon   1 confidant
   Plautine, confidente de Domitie   5 male characters

Psyché 1671
   Vénus   2 goddesses
   Aegiale ⎫
            ⎬ grâces   2 groups of suivantes
   Phaene ⎭   8 male characters
   Psyché
   Aglaure ⎫
            ⎬ soeurs de Psyché
   Cydippe ⎭

Pulchérie 1672
   Pulchérie, impératrice   3 noble ladies
   Irène, soeur de Léon   3 male characters
   Justine, fille de Martian

Suréna 1674
   Eurydice, fille d'Artabase, roi d'Arménie   3 noble ladies
   Ormène, dame d'honneur d'Eurydice   1 confidant
   Palmis, soeur de Suréna   4 male characters

    The quotations and references are based upon the Marty-Laveaux, edition of Corneille. Paris 1862-70. 12 vol. (Grands Écrivains de la France.)

PART I. CORNEILLE'S OWN THEORIES IN REGARD TO HIS HEROINES.

1. THEIR ARISTOCRATIC BIRTH.

The first point which strikes our attention, as we look over the long list of the female characters of Corneille is their aristocratic birth. Without exception they are of royal or noble family, and in this respect, they perpetuate a leading characteristic of the classic Greek tragedy, and at the same time conform to the ideals of the polite society of the seventeenth century in France. Nevertheless, it was only after a struggle that Corneille, himself a man of simple tastes and unostentatious mode of living, submitted to the aristocratic yoke. At heart he was of one mind with Diderot and Lessing, who in the next century waged such stubborn war against the exclusively aristocratic element in the French tragedy. Even in the seventeenth century, too, he had had a few examples of *bourgeois* tragedy to justify him in his position — Alexandre Hardy, the most unconventional dramatist of his time, and as such a horror later in the eyes of persons of quality, had introduced tragedies of a purely domestic nature upon the French stage, and had made a deep impression on Corneille. In discussing the nature of tragedy, Corneille says : « . . . j'ose m'imaginer que ceux qui ont restreint cette sorte de poème aux personnes illustres n'en ont décidé que sur l'opinion qu'ils ont eue qu'il n'y avoit que la fortune des rois et des princes qui fût capable d'une action telle que ce grand maître[1] de l'art nous prescrit. .... et je ne puis croire que l'hospitalité violée en la personne des filles de Scédase,[2] qui n'était qu'un paysan de Leuctres, soit moins digne d'elle que l'assassinat d'Agamemnon par sa femme ou la vengeance de cette mort par Oreste sur sa propre mère.»[3]

It is hard to realize that it is Corneille who is speaking. We imagine ourselves in the presence of a Diderot or a Lessing. Why then did not Corneille produce a *bourgeois* tragedy, which should be a masterpiece and take its place side by side with the aristocratic tragedies, which brought him immortal renown? There are several reasons. In the first place, two schools so opposed to each other could not thrive at the same time and as we know, the taste of the seventeenth century, under the influence of the Renaissance was purely aristocratic: secondly, there was a general feeling not only in France but in other countries, that only kings and queens were entitled to appear in tragedy. Scaliger[4] the century before had declared the only proper persons to be «reges, principes», and Opitz[5] in Germany under the influence of Scaliger, to be sure, had expressed the same opinion long before Gottsched became the apostle of the French classic tragedy across the Rhine. In Spain, Lope de Vega[6] had defined the royal character of the personages as one of the fundamental differences which distinguish tragedy from comedy.

Public sentiment was entirely in favor of the aristocratic

---

[1] Aristotle.
[2] See Hardy: *Scédase, ou l'Hospitalité Violée* in Le Théâtre d'Alexander Hardy, vol. I. Stengel edition. Marburg 1884.
[3] Épître à Monsieur de Zuylichem. See Oeuvres de Corneille V, p. 404.
[4] Julius Caesar Scaliger. Poetices I 6. Lyons 1561.
[5] Martini Opitii. Buch von der deutschen Poeterey. Breslau 1624.
[6] Lope de Vega. Rimas con el nuevo arte de hacer comedias. Madrid 1609.

tragedy, and yet Corneille ventured for once to defy the accepted canons of good taste. He introduced Don Sanche d'Aragon on the stage disguised as the son of an ordinary fisherman. — The aristocratic public of the year 1651 resented this intrusion, and refused to bestow serious attention on such a hero, even if he did prove at the end to be the king of Aragon. Such glorification of a menial looked like too great a menace to royalty. «Alors on avait à Paris les guerres de la Fronde, et l'on voyait en même temps briller à Londres un homme né obscur, prêt à mettre son titre de Milord Protecteur au dessus de celui des rois. On ne crut pas devoir encourager de tels exemples; et Don Sanche, fils d'un pêcheur ou cru tel dans la pièce, parut ressembler beaucoup trop à ce fils d'un brasseur de bière, devant qui tombaient ou pliaient les têtes couronnées. Cromwell tua Don Sanche».[1] And Corneille never again attempted to introduce a *bourgeois* element into the heroic drama. The «personne de notre condition à qui nous ressemblons tout à fait» was thus banished forever from the French classic stage. In adapting Maffei's *Mérope* to the French stage, Voltaire found himself forced to make numerous modifications to suit the cultivated taste of the eighteenth century, one of the most important being to eliminate the shocking idea of the Italian author in allowing his hero to be mistaken at first for a robber. Aristocrat through and through, Voltaire again, in criticising the *Julius Caesar* of Shakespeare, expressed it as his opinion that only an English audience would endure a chorus of artisans and Roman plebeians.[2] And Voltaire knew his nation. Royal or illustrious birth was a prime requisite of the heroes and heroines of the classic French tragedy.

Being of royal or illustrious birth, it is easy to see that the personages who figure in the dramas of Corneille had to

---

[1] François de Neufchâteau. L'Esprit du grand Corneille. Paris 1819.
[2] Voltaire. Discours sur la tragédie.

have royal or illustrious names, by which we must also
understand in the seventeenth century, names pleasing to French
ears. Conscientious worker that he was, even to the slightest
detail, Corneille deliberated long and carefully over this point.
Undoubtedly his sad experience with *Pertharite* made him
resolve to be more circumspect in future. Voltaire attributes
the failure of *Pertharite* to the revolting names, as he regards
them, of the personages. «Les noms seuls des héros de cette
pièce révoltent» he says: «c'est une Eduïge, un Grimoald,
un Unulphe .... Un Unulphe, un Grimoald annoncent d'ailleurs une tragédie bien lombarde. C'est une grande erreur de
croire que tous les noms barbares de Goths, de Lombards, de
Francs puissent faire sur la scène le même effet qu'Achille,
Iphigénie, Andromaque, Électre, Oreste, Pyrrhus. Boileau se
moque avec raison de celui qui pour son héros va choisir
Childebrand».[1] Perhaps some such comments at the time of the
fiasco of *Pertharite*, may have reached Corneille's ears. In any
case, on his return to the theatre, he speaks quite at length
on the subject of the names which he gave to his two original
heroines of *Sertorius*, Aristie and Viriate. In his remarks *Au
Lecteur*, he tells us that he changed the name of Antistie to
Aristie, because the latter was more pleasing to the ear. The
name of Viriate he invented on his own responsibility, deriving
it from the name of the illustrious Viriatus, king of Lusitania.
In like manner, Brueys,[2] fifteen years after Corneille's death,
showed his reverence for the teachings of the master by naming
one of his heroines Gabinie, after her father Gabinius, the
name of Susanna, handed down by history seeming to him not
to have «assez de noblesse pour le théâtre». The name of
Ildione in *Attila* passed through several transformations before
it reached its present state. Voltaire writes in his commentaries

---

[1] Voltaire. Remarques sur Pertharite.
[2] See Jusserand. Shakespeare en France in Cosmopolis for Nov. 1896.

«Corneille dans sa tragédie d'*Attila*, fait paraître Hildione, une princesse sœur d'un prétendu roi de France ; elle s'appelait Hildecone à la première représentation ; on changea en suite ce nom ridicule».[1] Marty-Laveaux inquires «Qu'eût-ce été si Corneille, au lieu d'adopter à peu près, en le francisant le nom d'Ildico, qui lui était donné par Priscus et Jornandès, eût connu les traditions du Nord et choisi les formes plus pures de Hiltgund, Hiltegunt, Hildegonde, qu'elles nous ont conservées».[2] Corneille, however, was quite right in softening down the name of his heroine, and above all in banishing the harsh guttural from it. The year 1667 had come, a new era had dawned. Racine was already in full competition with Corneille and had set a new fashion with his melodious Greek names.

Subordinate to the heroines of the classic French drama, were the confidants who followed in their train, a colorless set of personages, as far as the action of the play was concerned, but important as a piece of necessary paraphernalia. In the Greek tragedy, there were two kinds of confidant, the private confidant and the chorus, or public confidant. In the French tragedy, the the chorus continued to be employed by Jodelle, Garnier, Montchrestien and in a few pieces by Hardy, who nevertheless, declared it to be superfluous. In the drama of Corneille, the chorus does not appear, its functions being transferred to the confidant or suivante , who thus assumes the duties of the double set of characters in the Greek tragedy. These duties, however, are not very exacting. The confidant merely accompanies her mistress and interposes a remark here and there, that the heroine may rest from what would otherwise become a too long and fatiguing monologue. A very similar function is still seen in the confidants of the early operas

---

[1] Voltaire. Remarques sur Attila.
[2] Marty-Laveaux. Oeuvres de Corneille vol. VII p. 102.

of Verdi and Donizetti, who, in like manner, sing a judicious note now and then, to relieve the prima donna. The confidant of Corneille, by an occasional hint, also enables the heroine to change the theme of her conversation. Oftentimes too, a remark of the confidant is introduced to admit of one of those sharp pithy retorts, which are so characteristic of the drama of Corneille. The epoch-making «Moi!»[1] of *Médée* and the «Qu'il mourût!»[2] of *Horace* are made possible precisely by the naive question of the confidant. The force of the retort, the reaction, as it were, throws her back into her former insignificance.

In a small number of plays,[3] Corneille still allowed his confidant to recite the epic narration, which gathers up the threads of the tragedy, apprises the spectator of the downfall of the wrongdoer, or announces the tragic event which brings the play to a close. This prerogative of the confidant was highly approved of by Dryden, who, as an admirer of the French school, naturally shared the aversion of cultivated French people for a scene of bloodshed or violence on the open stage. And this, be it said, was a matter of no small consequence in the dramatic art of the seventeenth century in France.

The confidant of the Corneille tragedy was on the whole, however, hardly more than a lay figure, and thus she remained with but few exceptions, such as the Oenone of Racine's *Phèdre*, as long as the classic drama held sway on the French stage. That her very inertness was a mark of bienséance, can be seen by the severe manner of Voltaire, who reprimanded

---

[1] Médée 1 V 320.
[2] Horace 3 VI 1021.
[3] In Horace 3 II Julie announces the victory of Rome over Alba, and thus brings to an end the first of the double actions of which the play is composed; in Théodore 5' III, Stéphanie relates the death of Théodore, Didyme and Marcelle; in Suréna 5 V, Ormène announces the murder of Suréna.

Corneille severely for allowing two subalterns to open the play of *Rodogune*, and thus at the outset monopolize the attention of a public accustomed to be greeted by some pompous personage of the blood royal.

---

2. THE APPROPRIATE NUMBER.

The second point which a glance at the casts of Corneille's tragedies brings to our notice is the preponderance of plays introducing two heroines. Eighteen of the twenty-four dramas under consideration have two heroines, five have three heroines and one alone has but one heroine. It is, therefore evident that Corneille had a preference for two heroines, as the proper number. This is proved by his own words and by an examination of several plays in which his originality was especially drawn upon.

In working over the subject matter of *Sertorius*, Corneille was confronted by the absence of female characters. But he speedily surmounted this difficulty. «Comme il ne m'a fourni aucunes femmes,» he says «j'ai été obligé de recourir à l'invention pour en introduire *deux*, assez compatibles l'une et l'autre avec les vérités historiques à qui je me suis attaché. L'une a vécu de ce temps-là ; c'est la première femme de Pompée, qu'il répudia pour entrer dans l'alliance de Sylla, par le mariage d'Émilie, fille de sa femme. . . . . L'autre femme est une pure idée de mon esprit, mais qui ne laisse pas d'avoir aussi quelque fondement dans l'histoire. Elle nous apprend que les Lusitaniens appelèrent Sertorius d'Afrique pour être leur chef contre le parti de Sylla ; mais elle ne nous dit point, s'ils étaient en république ou sous une monarchie. Il n'y a donc rien qui répugne à leur donner une reine ; et je ne la pouvois faire sortir d'un rang plus considérable que celui de Viriatus, dont je lui fais porter le nom, le plus grand homme que l'Espagne ait opposé aux Romains, et le dernier, qui leur a fait tête dans ces provinces avant Sertorius.»[1]

From this quotation we see Corneille's preference for two heroines, between whom the spectator is called upon to divide his interest. At the same time we see the requirement of royal birth again in force.

The *Oedipe* of Corneille furnishes us with another example of the necessity of two heroines. In the Greek and Latin versions, where Jocaste is the only female figure, Corneille was disturbed by the absence of the love element. Love was not, as we shall see, the predominating element of his tragedy; indeed he was himself opposed to all sentimental love in tragedy. But he knew the taste of the French public and was therefore compelled to recognize the love element as one of the «principaux agréments, qui sont en possession de gagner la voix publique . . . Ces considérations m'ont fait . . . . introduire l'heureux épisode de Thésée et de Dircé»[2] this last character being introduced as the daughter of Jocaste.

Voltaire experienced the same difficulty as Corneille in treating the subject of Oedipus. Like Corneille, he had a sense of the fitness of things, and realized that there was no place in Sophocles' gloomy masterpiece for the introduction of a languishing love element. But as he tells us, he was obliged, in order to keep peace with the «amoureuse» of the troupe, to represent the tragic Jocaste, as complicated in an insipid love intrigue with Philoctète. Corneille got around this difficulty by his favorite device of introducing a second heroine for the purpose.

Likewise in *Sophonisbe*, notwithstanding the models furnished him in the previous works of Montchrestien (1596) and

---

[1] Sertorius. Au Lecteur.
[2] Examen d'Oedipe.

Mairet (1629), Corneille introduced in addition to the Carthaginian queen, celebrated in history, a rival heroine in the person of Éryxe, queen of Getulia, of whom he proudly says «C'est une reine de ma façon.»

Finally in the tragedy of *Tite et Bérénice*, which always invites comparison with the *Bérénice* of Racine, we find Corneille dividing the interest between two heroines. Racine's Bérénice stands alone; Corneille's heroine has a rival, Domitie, daughter of the emperor Corbulon.

The necessity of a dual heroine becomes apparent if we examine the construction of the Corneille tragedy and notice those points on which the poët laid the greatest stress. His favorite work was *Rodogune*, and he gives us the following reasons. «..Cette tragédie me semble être un peu plus à moi que celle qui l'ont précédée, à cause des incidents surprenants qui sont purement de mon invention; . . . certainement on peut dire que mes autres pièces ont peu d'avantages qui ne se rencontrent en celle-ci : elle a tout ensemble la beauté du sujet, la nouveauté des fictions; la force des vers, la facilité de l'expression, la solidité du raisonnement, la chaleur des passions, les tendresses de l'amour et de l'amitié; et cet heureux assemblage est ménagé de sorte qu'elle s'élève d'acte en acte.»[1] Here we find the requisites of a good tragedy according to Corneille, and that the complication of the plot was in his estimation one of its chief merits, can be seen by the complacency with which he speaks of *Héraclius*, a work so intricate as to be nearly unintelligible, and with perfect reason declared by Boileau to be a «logographe.»[2]

«Cette tragédie» he says «a encore plus d'invention que celle de Rodogune, . . . le poème est si embarrassé qu'il demande une merveilleuse attention. J'ai vu de fort bons esprits, et des personnes des plus qualifiées de la cour, se plaindre

---

[1] Examen de Rodogune.
[2] Bolaeana 1742 p. 111.

de ce que sa représentation fatiguait autant l'esprit qu'une étude sérieuse.»[1] Thus we see that a complicated plot was regarded as an essential in Corneille's dramatic system. And the complicated plot naturally brought with it a complicated set of characters; hence the two heroines, standing face to face and taxing the divided sympathies of the spectator. We have already compared the two Bérénice tragedies of 1670. It is precisely in the simplicity of the version of Racine that the work of the younger poet distinguishes itself from the drama of Corneille. Racine had no sympathy for the methods of Corneille in this respect. In the preface to his tragedy, he refers slightingly, though without mentioning any names, to his illustrious predecessor. «Il n'y a que le vraisemblable que touche dans la tragédie. Et qu'elle vraisemblance y a-t-il qu'il arrive en un jour une multitude de choses, qui pourraient à peine arriver en plusieurs semaines? Il y en a qui pensent que cette simplicité est une marque de peu d'invention. Ils ne songent pas qu'au contraire toute l'invention consiste à faire quelque chose de rien et que tout ce grand nombre d'incidents a toujours été le refuge des poètes qui ne sentoient dans leur génie ni assez d'abondance ni assez de force pour attacher durant cinq actes leurs spectateurs par une action simple soutenue de la violence des passions, de la beauté des sentiments et de l'élégance de l'expression.»[2]

But in simplifying the construction of the tragedy of Corneille, in banishing what he would perhaps have regarded as the superfluous second heroine, Racine would have been making too radical a change in the drama of Corneille. The two heroines introduced by Corneille had other reasons for existence, as we shall see, if we consider the methods which the poet used, of having them appear to the best advantage.

[1] Examen d'Heraclius.
[2] Racine. Préface de Bérénice 1670.

What are the most striking scenes in which Corneille's female characters appear? The student of the classic tragedy will recognize them at once as the monologues, the scenes of complaint between the heroine and her confidant, and those peculiar scenes, where the two heroines meet to defy each other, to overwhelm each other with magnanimity, or to discuss some fine point, in which they can display their skill in argument.

Let us consider the eight following works with reference to these special features: *Le Cid*, as the masterpiece of Corneille and the one on which his fame rests; *Horace*, the first tragedy purely «cornélienne»; *Rodogune*, the poet's favorite work; *Pertharite*, the failure of which caused his temporary retirement from the theatre; *Oedipe*, the work with which he returned to theatre; *Sertorius*, the work, in which the creation of female characters drew entirely on the poet's powers of invention. *Tite et Bérénice*, the piece in which the tragic methods of Corneille and Racine came into competition; *Suréna*, the last play of Corneille.

In *Le Cid*, we find the following relations:
Chimène confers with her confidant 1 I, 3 III, 5 IV.
The Infante confers with hers 1 II, 2 V, 5 III.
The two confer together 2 III, 4 II,
The Infante has a monologue 1 III, 5 II.
Chimène has no monologue, the one which Rodrigue delivers describing Chimène's state of mind as well as his own.

In *Horace*:
Sabine confers with her confidant, 1 I, 3 II.
Camille confers with hers, 1 II.
Sabine and Camille confer together, 3 III, 3 IV.
Sabine has a monologue, 3 I.
Camille has a monologue, 4 IV.

In *Rodogune*:
Rodogune confers with a confidant, 1 V.

— 32 —

Cléopatre confers with her confidant, 2 II, 4 IV, 5 II.
Rodogune and Cléopatre come together, 5 IV.
Rodogune has a monologue, 3 III.
Cléopatre has a monologue, 2 I, 4 V, 4 VII, 5 I.

In *Pertharite:*
Rodelinde has no confidant.
Eduïge has no confidant.
Rodelinde and Éduïge defy each other 1 II, 3 II, 5 III.
No monologues.

In *Oedipe:*
Dircé confers with her confidant 2 II, 2 III.
Jocaste has no scene with her confidant.
Dircé and Jocaste come together 3 II.
Dircé has a monologue 3 I.

In *Sertorius:*
Viriate confers with her confidant, 2 I, 2 III.
Aristie has no confidant.
Viriate and Aristie come together, 5 I.
No monologues.

In *Tite et Bérénice:*
Domitie conplains to her confidant, 1 I, 2 VII.
Bérénice confers with her minister, 3 IV, 4 I.
Domitie and Bérénice come together, 3 III.
No monologues.

In *Suréna:*
Eurydice confers with her confidant, 1 I, 4 I.
Palmis has no confidant.
Eurydice and Palmis come together, 1 II, 4 II, 5 IV.
No monologues.

A comparison of the plays in the above scheme shows us that, whereas Corneille was more or less variable in his application of monologues and scenes with confidants, the scene between the two rival heroines became a fixed part of his system. The very nature of the Corneille drama required the the heroines to meet and fence with each other, so to speak, before the play could come to a satisfactory *dénoument*.[1]

In the matter of monologues, more liberty was possible. Corneille allowed himself to be governed by the prevailing tendencies. In his early dramas, they are frequent enough. The actors desired them, because they thought that they offered superior opportunities for the display of their talents. Thus it was that Émilie opens the tragedy of *Cinna*, with a long and spirited monologue of fifty two lines, a defiant tirade threatening the life of Augustus, which, it is easy to see, must have met with the unbounded approval of the ambitious women of the Fronde.

But on the whole, monologues disappeared gradually from the works of Corneille, as well as from those of the later classic dramatists. *La Thébaide* and the *Phédre* of Racine offer some of the last monologues to be found in the classic tragedy. Actors and dramatists alike would seem to have come over to the opinion of Hardy, who, long before Corneille's day, had done his best to do away with monologues which hindered the movement of the play, and contributed to it nothing but wearisome monotony. Voltaire even tells us that the actresses in his time had ceased to recite the monologue of Émilie, to which we have referred, and that he was obliged to insist upon the restoration of it, on account of the many beauties which it contains.[2]

The scenes between the two heroines, however, could not be so easily spared. Although in themselves they are often-

---

[1] For further instances see Pompée 5 II, Théodore 2 IV, Héraclius 2 I, 2 III, 2 VII, Andromède 3 II, Nicomède 5 VI, La Toison d'Or 3 IV, Sophonisbe 1 III, 3 II, 5 IV, Othon 4 IV, Agésilas 2 VII, 4 IV, Attila 3 III, Psyché 4 V, Pulchérie 3 II, 5 I.

[2] Remarques sur Cinna.

times mere scenes of conversation, to use the expression of Voltaire,[1] who condemned them as such, they nevertheless possessed the advantage of bringing two aristocratic ladies to gether in such a way as to allow them to shine in their own reflection and indirectly suggest by their sallies the brilliant women of the salons of the times. In the proud self consciousness, too, with which they assert themselves, they embody the spirit of the age.

Corneille had two methods of treating the scenes between his heroines, the long tirade and the pithy dialogue. The first is well illustrated by the scene between his two original heroines in Sertorius 5 I. Aristie begins with a tirade of thirty two lines, Viriate replies with one of twenty seven; Aristie then has one line which allows Viriate to take up the retort closing the scene with a tirade of nineteen lines.

The second method, that of breaking up the line into short pithy utterances, which sometimes admit of two remarks and two retorts, all within the fixed number of syllables, is well shown by two examples in *Sophonisbe*. The first is in the scathing tone of high comedy.

Sophonisbe.
Avez-vous en ces lieux, quelque commerce?

Éryxe.
Aucun.

Sophonisbe.
D'où le savez-vous donc?

D'un peu de sens commun:
Sophonisbe 1 III 169-70.

The second is in the heroic style in which Corneille excelled, and in which his original queen, Éryxe, appeared to special advantage.

Sophonisbe.
Vous parlez un peu haut.

---

[1] Remarques sur Sertorius, See 5 I.

> Éryxe.
>> Je suis amante et reine.
>
> Sophonisbe.
> Et captive, de plus.
>
> Éryxe.
>> On va briser ma chaîne;
> Et la captivité ne peut abattre un cœur
> Qui se voit assuré de celui du vainqueur:
>
>> *Sophonisbe* 1 III 227-30.

These scenes became a fixed part of the French classic system. The famous «Moi!» of *Médée*, coming with volcanic force at the end of an otherwise harmless Alexandrine verse uttered by the confidant, had proved the efficacy of this device in tragedy.

This terse dialogue, however, was not an invention of Corneille. His predecessors had made use of it, though not with the same telling effect. To find the sources of it, it is necessary to go back to the beginnings of French poetry. In the earliest French drama extant, the Mystère d'Adam, an Anglo-Norman play of the end of the twelfth century, we find the temptation of Adam and Eve developed as follows:

Eve begins:
> Manjue, Adam, ne sez que est
> pernum ço bien que nus est prest
> *Adam.* Est il tant bon? *Eva.* Tu le savras
> nel poez saver, si'n gusteras
> *Adam.* j'en duit. *Eva.* lai le. *Adam.* n'en feras pas
> *Eva.* del demorer fais tu que las
> *Adam.* E jol prendrai. *Eva.* manjue t'en
> par ce savras e mal e bien
> jon manjerai premirement
> *Adam* E je apres. *Eva.* Seurement.
>> *Mystère d'Adam*, Edition Lagarche, Tours 1854; Edition Palustre, Paris 1877.

As another example of the fondness for this vivacious style of conversation in mediaeval poetry, let us quote the meeting between Alexandre and King Artus in the *Cligès* of Chrestien de Troies.

«Don estes vos?» — «De Grece somes»
«De Grece?» — «Voire.» — «Qui'st tes père?»
«Par ma foi, sire, l'anperere.»
«Et comant as non, biaux amis?»
«Alexandre me fu nous mis
La ou je recui sel et cresme
Et crestanté et batesme.»

Chrestien de Troies. *Cligès* 366-72.
Edition Förster, Halle 1888.

These two examples, the one taken from the earliest French drama, the other from the most famous French poet of the Middle Ages, show us that Corneille in his application of terse dialogue, was simply, perpetuating a national characteristic, which had existed from the beginnings of French poetry. And at the time, when he began to write, when the women of France were commencing to attract so much attention in literary and political life, he could not apply these conversations to better advantage or with more flattering results than by allowing his two heroinès to show their wit and cleverness by means of them.

We are not to assume, however, that the two heroines in the tragedy of Corneille were always of the same importance. We, know indeed, that the rôle of the Infante in the *Cid* is of so decidedly secondary importance, that it is usually omitted altogether from the representation, as superfluous and a detriment to the piece. In the Spanish original, the Infante had been a formidable rival to Jimena, and had even put on Rodrigo's spurs for him, when he went forth to war. Of course such an action on the part of a princess of the blood royal would not have been in keeping with the French ideals of *bienséance* in the classic tragedy. The rôle of Livie also disappeared from the tragedy of *Cinna*, and her best line was put into the mouth of Émilie. But on the whole, it was Corneille's preference to invest each heroine with the same importance, as we shall see, if we examine the play in which his originality was most drawn upon. We have indicated that in *Sertorius*, Corneille introduced two female characters of his own invention. These two women are so counterbalanced against each other that Hémon summarizes the play briefly and justly as follows: «Premier acte: Aristie. Second acte: Viriate, Troisième acte: Aristie. Quatrième acte: Viriate. Le cinquième acte nous montrera les deux héroines réunies».[1] This tendency on the part of Corneille is but another example of the poet's love of symmetry. The mathematical accuracy with which the heroines of *Sertorius* are introduced, is thoroughly in keeping with the system of the poet in general. A fixed number of acts,[2] a fixed number of lines, a fixed number of rhymes, a fixed number of personages, — all these elements combined to make the dramatic system of Corneille.

---

3. THE IDEAL TYPE.

Having now established the fact that Corneille's preference was for two heroines of noble birth, we turn to a consideration of the qualities of character, which he deemed most appropriate for them as heroines of tragedy. We are naturally predisposed to imagine a heroine as being in love with the hero. We expect to find the passion of love predominant in the relations between the sexes, precipitating the action of the drama according to the accompanying circumstances. We think of the

---

[1] Hémon. Théâtre de Pierre Corneille vol. IV p. 415. Paris 1887.

[2] Corneille divided his tragedies, with the exception of *Agésilas* into five acts, the first corresponding to the prologue, the second, third, and fourth to the episode, and the fifth to the exode of the Greek tragedy. He wrote *Agésilas* in three acts and in *vers libres*, innovations which did not prove successful. Racine wrote but one piece *Esther*, in three acts; Voltaire, several tragedies among others *La Mort de César*.

heroine, too, as a woman, a feminine creature, with feminine impulses, but we are far from comprehending the women of Corneille. Scattered throughout his writings, we find many utterances bearing more or less directly on the subject, from which we see that his ideal of a tragic heroine was not a Juliet, a Francesca or a Margaret.

In speaking of tragedy in general, he says «Sa dignité demande quelque grand intérêt d'État, ou quelque passion, plus noble et plus mâle que l'amour, telles que sont *l'ambition* ou *la vengeance* . . . . Il est à propos d'y mêler l'amour, parce qu'il a toujours beaucoup d'agrément et peut servir de fondement à ces intérêts, et à ces autres passions dont je parle; mais il faut qu'il ce contente du second rang dans le poëme et leur laisse le premier».[1]

The Corneille heroine is, therefore, not to be carried away by any uncontrollable passion of love. She is rather to have at heart the interest of the State, to be moved by political ambition and to seek revenge for the wrongs which she may have suffered. There is nothing distinctively feminine in these traits of character, though they are possible.

These opinions were expressed by Corneille in 1660, before Racine had appeared upon the scene to win all hearts with his tragic masterpieces, founded on the passion of love. Corneille's contempt for this weakness was called out by the continued success which the love tragedies of Quinault had been meeting with during those seven years when he was absent from the theatre.

In a private letter to St. Evremond after the failure of *Sophonisbe*, Corneille complains bitterly at the change which had undeniably come about in the taste of the public. «J'ai cru, jusques ici, que l'amour était une passion trop chargée de faiblesse pour être la dominante dans une pièce héroique et

---

[1] Discours du poëme dramatique.

j'aime qu'elle y serve d'ornement et non pas de corps et que les grands âmes ne la laissent agir, qu'autant qu'elle est compatible avec de plus nobles impressions. Nos doucereux et nos enjoués sont de contraire avis».[1] And as sample of a model heroine from an ethical and heroic point of view, Corneille cites this same Sophonisbe, of whom he says «Je lui prête un peu d'amour; mais elle règne sur lui, et ne daigne l'écouter qu'autant qu'il peut servir à ces passions dominantes qui régnent sur elle, et à qui elle sacrifie toutes les tendresses de son coeur, Massinisse, Syphax, sa propre vie. — J'aime mieux qu'on me reproche d'avoir fait mes femmes trop héroïnes, par une ignorante et basse affectation de les faire ressembler aux originaux qui en sont venues jusqu'à nous, que de m'entendre louer d'avoir efféminé mes héros par une docte et sublime complaisance au goût de nos délicats, qui veulent de l'amour partout.»[2]

It is therefore clear, that it was not Corneille's purpose to sacrifice his heroines on the altar of love. But it was not entirely of his own accord that he had come to these views, which he expressed after the failure of *Sophonisbe*. If we go back to the *«Sentiments de l'Academie Française sur la tragicomédie du Cid»*, we shall find that Corneille was rebuked by this body for allowing Chimène to yield to her love for Rodrigue. In a moment of weakness, she admits her love for the hero. The Académie maintained that Rodrigue should have been the one to yield, that he should have allowed his love to triumph over his duty, and that the heroine should have gallantly been permitted to hold her supremacy to the end. As we have said, Corneille was ever ready to take suggestions, if he found that they came from a recognized authority, and perhaps this is why in the long list of his tragedies, we find

---

[1] Lettre à M. de Saint Évremond 1666.
[2] Sophonisbe. Au Lecteur.

the women dominating, domineering over the men. Cinna had every reason to call his beloved Emilie an «aimable inhumaine».[1]

— In discussing the character of Flaminius in *Nicomède*, Corneille reveals to us another idea, which influenced him in the development of his characters, that of embodying in them some abstract quality or historical meaning. Flaminius, for instance, stands for the imperious foreign policy of the Roman senate under the republic, 180 B. C. As Corneille says «C'est le caractère que j'ai donné à leur république en la personne de leur ambassadeur Flaminius.»[2] It is not to be supposed, however, that the great public were conscious of any abstract significance in the personages in Corneille's tragedies. They could hardly be held responsible for the political transactions of Rome in the Orient. It was only the more cultivated, who were expected to read between the lines. Balzac, it will be remembered, showed his superior perspicacity by seeing in Émilie the very embodiment of the passion of liberty at Rome.

One other trait of characters peculiar to Corneille remains to be spoken of, the striving for admiration on the part of his heroes and heroines. Of Nicomède the poet says «Ce héros de ma façon sort un peu des règles de la tragédie, en ce qu'il ne cherche point à faire pitié par l'excès de ses malheurs, mais le succès a montré, que la fermeté des grands coeurs, qui n'excite que l'admiration dans l'âme du spectateur, est quelquefois aussi agréable que la compassion que notre art nous commande de mendier pour leurs misères.»[3] The heroine of Corneille must, therefore, command admiration.

Such are the requisites of the heroine of Corneille, as we gather them from among the scattering remarks of the poet. Corneille does not formulate his ideas in a single chapter of

---

[1] Cinna 3 III, 905.
[2] *Nicomède*. Au Lecteur.
[3] ibid.

concisely expressed rules. He leaves us to take note of his remarks in passing and to prove them by observing the application of them in his dramatic works. It will, therefore, be worth our while, before entering upon à detailed examination of the plays themselves to state once more briefly the ideas of Corneille.

His ideal heroine must first compel the admiration of the spectator by her devotion to her country. She must be guided in her choice of a husband by unbounded personal ambition, and she must be possessed of keen political insight.

Secondly, she must have an abstract or historical significance, apart from representing merely a being of flesh and blood.

Finally she must be inspired by revenge in the solution of the problem which places her in the drama.

In the above order, let us see with what consistency Corneille applied his theories in practice. First as to the patriotic, ambitious, political character of his heroines.

The first heroine, who appears on the scene, the Créuse[1] of *Médée*, refuses to bestow her hand on her lover, fearing that such an alliance might not conduce to the good of the State. Chimène[2] demands the punishment of Rodrigue for the welfare of the commonwealth. In the interest of her country too, she becomes reconciled to his pardon.[3] The good of the State, the welfare of the fatherland are likewise, kept in view by other heroines of Corneille.

---

[1] Et vous reconnoîtrez que je ne vous préfère
Que le bien de *l'État*, mon pays et mon père.
Médée 2 V 673—4.

[2] Immolez, disje, Sire, au bien de tout *l'État*
Tout ce qu'enorgueillit un si haut attentat,
Le Cid 2 VIII 695—6.

[3] Rodrigue a des vertus que je ne puis haïr;
. . . .
Rodrigue à *l'État* devient si nécessaire,
Le Cid 5 VII 1803—9.

Andromède,[1] Dircé,[2] Sophonisbe[3] and Pulchérie[4] unite in glorifying the idea of dying for their countries sake. The love of country coupled with personal ambition is well illustrated by the Infante,[5] who overcomes her secret passion for Rodrigue by the reflection that any other than a monarch would be unworthy of her hand. Her example is followed by a long line of heroines who concur in expressing the same opinion. Laodice,[6] Dircé,[7] Viriate,[8] Elpinice,[9] Aglatide,[10] Honorie[11] and

---

[1] Heureuse, ...
 Si le salut public peut naître de ma perte!
 Malheureuse . . . .
 . . . . . . que je ne suis, pas la première et l'unique
 Qui rende à votre État la sûreté publique!
Andromède 2 IV 692—9.

[2] Il est encore plus doux de *mourir pour son roi.*
Oedipe 2 III 638.

[3] J'immolai ma tendresse *au bien de ma patrie:*
Sophonisbe 1 II 43.

[4] Je sacrifierai tout au bonheur de *l'État.*
Pulchérie 4 II 1224.

[5] Tout autre qu'un monarque est indigne de moi.
Le Cid 1 II 100.

[6] Je suis reine, seigneur; . . . .
 . . . . la reine d'Arménie
 Est due à l'héritier du roi de Bithynie,
Nicomède 1 I 57—64.

[7] Et jamais sur ce coeur on n'avancera rien
 Qu'en me donnant un sceptre, ou me rendant le mien.
Oedipe 2 I 495—96.

[8] . . . . le glorieux dessein
 De m'affermir au trône en lui donnant la main :
Sertorius 2 I 391—2.

[9] Cotys est roi, ma soeur . . . .
 . . . .
 Assuré de mon coeur *que son trône lui donne,*
Agésilas 1 II 11—13.

[10] Et lorsqu'on vous destine *un roi* pour votre époux,
 J'en veux un aussi bien que vous.
Agésilas 1 I 51—52.

[11] Enfin, je veux *un roi:*
Attila 2 II 490.

Pulchérie,[1] in marrying are all imbued with the passion of self-aggrandizement. The ambition of Cleopâtre[2] is to be mistress of the world, even if for only a day. The aim of the Pulchérie[3] of 1647 is to see the whole world at her feet. Cleopâtre[4] tells us that princes do not deign to yield to the voice of love. This sentiment is taken up by Mandane[5] and echoed again by the Pulchérie[6] of 1672. Dircé[7] denounces the match planned for her by her step-father as a political scheme. Aristie[8] proudly boasts that her attempts to charm the old hero Sertorius are merely made in the interests of politics. And finally as if to establish once for all the true ideal of a tragic heroine, according to Corneille, Mandane cries out:

N'aimons plus que par politique
Agésilas 4 II 1439.

It is perfectly true, as Hémon repeatedly shows, that the later plays of Corneille degenerated into mere political tangles,

---

[1] Il falloit m'apporter la main *d'un empéreur*,
Pulchérie 3 III 924.

[2] Ne durât-il qu'un jour, ma gloire est sans seconde
D'être du moins un jour la maîtresse du monde,
Pompée 2 I 429—30.

[3] Je sais qu'il m'appartient, ce trône où tu te sieds,
Que c'est à moi d'y voir tout le monde à mes pieds;
Héraclius 1 II 143—4.

[4] Charmion
L'amour certes sur vous a bien peu de puissance.
Cléopatre
Les princes ont cela de leur haute naissance.
Pompée, 2 I 369—70.

[5] Mais un grand coeur doit être au dessus de l'amour.
Agésilas, 4 II 1421.

[6] Le trône met une âme au-dessus des tendresses
Pulchérie 1 I 114.

[7] J'ai vu sa politique . . . .
. . . . Politique nouvelle!
Oedipe 2 II 526—30.

[8] . . . . en cet hymen l'amour n'a point de part,
Qu'il n'est qu'un pur effet de noble politique,
Sertorius 1 III 328—9.

in which it does not seem to be the poet's object to interest the heart of a spectator. Politics form the basis of the entire play; the heroines seem to have no other idea in mind. Although this characteristic is peculiar to the later plays, it is no new feature in them. We have already indicated the touch of politics in *Médée* and the *Cid*. We have only to examine in order each and every play which belongs to the first period of Corneille to find that the political germ was there from the first and had an irresistible attraction for Corneille.

In *Horace* Sabine[1] subdues her emotions as a wife by reflecting that the contest between Alba and Rome is necessary for the good of the State. Camille[2] likewise expresses her admiration for her father for placing the welfare of Rome above the personal happiness of his daughter. Emilie,[3] though apparently avenging a personal wrong in seeking the life of Augustus, does not neglect to make it clear that it is her chief work to free Rome from imperial rule, and to set up a republican form of government. The empress Livie[4] declares that even a murder is justifiable if it be committed on behalf of the State. The confidant Stratonice[5] shudders as she sees in the Christian martyr Polyeucte an enemy to the State.

---

[1] Rome, ...
. . . .
Je sais que ton *Etat* encore en sa naissance.
Ne sauroit sans la guerre, affermir sa puissance;
Horace 1 I 33—40.

[2] Ne préfère-t-il point *l'Etat* à sa famille?
Ne regarde-t-il point Rome plus que sa fille?
Horace 1 III 255—56.

[3] «Et faisons publier par toute l'Italie:
La liberté de Rome est l'oeuvre d'Émilie: . .»
Cinna 1 II 109—110.

[4] Tous ces crimes *d'Etat* qu'on fait pour la couronne.
Le ciel nous en absout alors qu'il nous la donne,
Cinna 5 II 1609—10.

[5] C'est l'ennemi commun de *l'Etat* et des dieux,
Polyeucte 3 II 780.

Cléopâtre[1] assures her twin sons that her constant striving has been to establish them firmly on the throne; Rodogune[2] regards herself as a victim to the cause of her country. Dona Isabelle[3] frankly confesses that she marries simply because she deems such a step necessary to the good of the State.

In a word the heroines of Corneille one and all are thoroughly tinctured with politics. It is therefore, but a step farther to see in them a series of abstract symbols, representing certain political phases in history. Desjardins[4] has shown that Corneille's dramas taken together form a connected history of Rome from the earliest times down to the barbaric invasions in the fifth century. As Corneille himself tells us that he purposely made Flaminius represent the foreign policy of the Roman senate under the republic, and as Balzac, as we have said, had called Émilie the very embodiment of the passion of liberty, it is quite probable that Corneille always did keep the abstract political significance of his heroines in mind. It is a common objection to them, as a class, that they are lacking in the real qualities of the concrete human being.

From the point of view of Desjardins, *Horace* treats of those days in the history of Rome, which established forever the supremacy of the eternal city about 660 B. C. Camille would, therefore, represent Rome and Sabine Alba Longa.

Sophonisbe deals with the Punic Wars and the political policy of Rome in Africa 203 B. C. Sophonisbe represents the soul of Carthage and the patriotism of the family of Barca.

---

[1] Pour vous sauver *l'Etat*, que n'eusse-je pu faire ?
Rodogune 2 III 539.

[2] Je suivois mon destin en victime *d'Etat*.
Rodogune 3 III 874.

[3] Mais l'amour de *l'Etat*, plus fort que de moi-même,
Cherche, au lieu de l'objet le plus doux à mes yeux,
Le plus digne héros de régner en ces lieux ;
Don Sanche 2 II 566—68.

[4] Desjardins. Le Grand Corneille Historien. Paris 1861.

Éryxe is the personification of Africa jealous of the supremacy of Carthage.

Nicomède deals with the foreign policy of the Roman senate under the Republic 180 B. C. Laodice queen of Armenia associated together with the hero Nicomède, personifies the spirit of heroic opposition to the increasing power of Rome abroad.

Sertorius deals with the civil wars 79 B. C. Aristie represents the Roman aristocracy. Viriate stands for the liberty of Spain. *Suréna* tréats of the same epoch and represents the stubborn resistance of the Parthian Empire against the encroachments of Rome. Suréna, the conqueror of Crassus in 53 B. C. together with Eurydice, personifies this stubborn resistance.

Pompée deals with the events following the defeat of Pompey at Pharsalia 48 B. C. Cornélie, widow of Pompey,[8] represents the Roman aristocracy, Cléopatre the ambition of Egypt.

Cinna deals with the foundation of the Roman Empire about 10 B. C. Émilie represents the opposition to Augustus, the spirit of liberty with which the republican aristocracy were imbued.

Othon treats of the military revolution which followed the fall of the Augustan family 68 A. D. In this play, Plautine and her lover Othon stand for the old empire triumphing by aid of the pretorian guard. Camille, niece of Galba, represents the tendency to a re-establishment of the republic.

In *Tite et Bérénice* we find Rome under the Flavian dynasty. Bérénice is the impersonation of Judea.

In *Polyeucte* we behold in the hero and his wife Pauline the dawn of Christianity at Rome 250 A. D.

Théodore in the reign of Diocletian, 284—305, is the personification of religious martyrdom, Marcelle representing the spirit of religious persecution.

In the Pulchérie of 1672, we see the remnants of the proud spirit of Rome in the period between the commencement of the barbaric invasions and the coming of Attila 414—451.

In *Attila* is represented the overwhelming invasion of the Northern tribes. Honorie impersonates the fall of Rome, Ildione the rise of Gaule, of that fair France which Corneille was destined see at the height of her glory.

In the foregoing scheme, we thus have a more or less connected series of the various phases and epochs of Roman history, represented by the heroines of Corneille. It is a question, however, whether Corneille had the idea in mind at the outset of his career, to reproduce the history of Rome on the stage. To be sure, his first original piece, *Horace*, would seem to indicate the beginnings of such a scheme dealing as it does, with the earliest events in Roman history. But his next piece is by no means a continuation of such a plan. *Cinna*, as is well known, deals with events which took place nearly seven hundred and fifty years later. Furthermore, *Sophonisbe*, the play which stands next in chronological order to *Horace*, though at a long distance, was not written until twenty-three years after the production of *Horace*. And it should be remembered that Corneille, in the meantime, had abandoned playwriting for ever, as he himself supposed, in 1652. It is more reasonable to suppose that Corneille was attracted to Rome rather than to Greece as his scene of action, by the very nature of Roman history, extending as it did from 753 B. C. down into the Middle Ages to 476 A. D. and furnishing an infinitely greater wealth and variety of historic material than did the history of ancient Greece, which came to an end long before the Christian era. Further, Corneille must have found an extraordinary charm in the insatiable political ambition of Rome; for this is the character with which he most pronouncedly endowed his heroines. Even in *Oedipe* which in the grand and gloomy original has not the remotest resemblance to the political tragedy of Corneille, he could not resist the temptation to introduce a scheming political princess though he claims to have created the character of Dircé in order to introduce the necessary love episode, to which his public had become accustomed. Be that as it may, Corneille would seem to have been unable to draw the line between love and politics. Pauline is his only heroine who portrays to us in a convincing manner a faithful wife, and a woman.

— The remaining plays of Corneille fall out of the Roman scheme, but that does not prevent the heroines who appear in them from embodying some general political idea, and as a rule, they personify some noble idea. The women in Corneille's later plays, even though rivals, fairly overwhelm each other with magnanimity. A notable exception, however to the lofty type of character developed by Corneille is to be found in the Cléopatre of *Rodogune*. Lessing was right in calling her a monster. She certainly was the personification of «la passion du pouvoir poussée jusqu'à la rage et jusqu'au crime.»[1]

— The third element, which Corneille introduced into his heroines, was the thirst for revenge. In the seeking of glorious revenge for wrongs suffered, the poet found what he regarded as an ideal means of making his women heroic. In this particular, the heroines of Corneille would seem to take on a genuinely tragic aspect, for the poet gives most of them a problem which, according to the heroine's idea, can only be solved by the shedding of blood. Corneille employed two methods of revenge, by which the heroine might solve her problem in a way which should redound to her glory. According to the first method, the heroine declares that she will marry the man who will avenge her wrongs; according to the second, she undertakes the revenge herself without the intervention of a third

---

[1] Petit de Julleville. Le Théatre en France. 1889, p. 121.

person. The intention of the heroine would, therefore seem to be tragic. The spectator not versed in the Corneille tragedy begins to anticipate a thrilling action. And here it should be said that we must not spend too much time in insisting on the purely abstract side of the Corneille tragedy and its heroines. There is no doubt the poet found a great charm in investing his characters with a hidden meaning, but if we read the Examens of Corneille, we cannot but see that he regarded himself primarily as dramatist. His heroes undoubtedly stood for abstract or political ideas in many cases, and by the élite of society in the seventeenth century they were appreciated and enjoyed as such. But to the mass of theatre goers, unversed in Roman history, the plays of Corneille were regarded merely as plays. Indeed, as the poet himself freely confesses, he took great liberties with history for the sake of making an effective play,[1] and in this method of procedure he was followed by Racine and Voltaire. Dryden[2] also expresses great admiration for Corneille's skill in manipulating the facts of history. Corneille availed himself to the full extent of the poet's license, and in more than one place he refers to the ignorance of the public in matters of history and geography, and thereby excuses himself for what might otherwise seem to be a too bold abuse of poetic license on his part. In speaking of the change, which he sometimes made in the circumstances of history, Corneille says: «Il y a quelque apparence de présumer que la mémoire de l'auditoire, qui les aura lues autrefois ne s'y sera pas si fort attachée qu'il s'aperçoive assez du changement.»[3]

Again in discussing the changes necessitated by the dramatization of the historical matter of *Sertorius* Corneille

---

[1] Examen de Rodogune.
[2] Dryden. Essay of Dramatic Poesy 1668.
[3] Discours de la Tragédie.

speaks of «l'auditeur, qui communément n'a qu'une teinture superficielle de l'histoire.»[1]

— We see therefore, that Corneille's object was to make an effective and interesting play. Leaving aside, therefore, the abstract element in his heroines, let us consider them as concrete human beings of flesh and blood. Bear in mind that the heroines of Corneille have in common one glorious ideal, the preservation and enhancement of their honor (gloire), and they compel admiration by the boldness with which they seek their revenge.

We have called attention to two methods by which Corneille allows his heroines to solve their problem. Let us see his manner of applying them in his dramas, and begin with his most famous heroine.

Chimène is a young Spanish girl. She stands in conflict between her love for Rodrigue, and her duty, which requires her to avenge the death of her father, slain at the hand of of Rodrigue to avenge the death of his father. How does she solve her problem? What is the heroic moment in which she compels the admiration of the spectator? It is the moment when, sacrificing everything to her duty, she comes to a full realization of her own worth by making her hand the reward to the one who shall bring her the head of Rodrigue. To the king she says:

> A tous vos cavaliers *je demande sa tête:*
> Oui, qu'un d'eux me l'apporte, et je suis sa conquête;
> . . . .
> J'épouse le vainqueur, si Rodrigue est puni.
>
> *Le Cid* 4 V 1401—4.

This is, therefore, the culminating point, the heroic moment in the character of Chimène. These are the lines which make one shudder, to use the expression of Mme. de Sévigné,

---

[1] Sertorius. Au Lecteur.

the lines which announce the arrival on the scene of a new type of tragic heroine. Chimène quite outdazzled the other heroines, who were competing for public favor in the year 1636. The Sophonisbe of Mairet, the Cléopatre of Benserade, the Mariamne of Tristan l'Hermite were cast in the shade; The condemnation of Chimène at the hands of Scudery and the Académie was of no avail, for as Boileau tells us:

> En vain contre le Cid un ministère se ligue
> Tout Paris pour Chimène a les yeux de Rodrigue
>
> Satire IX.

Corneille borrowed this solution which Chimène brings to bear on her problem directly from the Spanish original of Castro. That it impressed him as eminently appropriate for a heroïne of tragedy, can be seen by examining his subsequent dramas. In *Cinna* we find a young Roman girl harassed as Chimène was by conflicting emotions. Her inclination prompts her to accept the offer of marriage made her by her lover but her duty requires her to avenge the death of her father proscribed some twenty years before by the Emperor Augustus. How does she solve her problem? After due deliberation, and without doubt, influenced by the great success of Chimène, Corneille decided to allow her to solve her problem in the same way, and Émilie therefore, makes her entrance upon the scene with her mind made up. To her confidant she says:

> Quoique j'aime Cinna, quoique mon coeur l'adore,
> S'il me veut posséder, Auguste doit périr:
> *Sa tête est le seul prix* dont il peut m'acquérir.
>
> *Cinna* 1 II 54—56.

Was Emilie a success? Did she realize the ideal of the great ladies before whom she appeared? It would seem so. Only a few years later, Mme. de Chevreuse, with the boldness of an Émilie, organized a conspiracy for the assassination of Cardinal Mazarin. In any case, from a theatrical point of view, Corneille was quite right in thinking that he had hit upon a device, which it was worth while to bear in mind for future use; indeed he was so much impressed with the idea, that in Rodogune, his favorite work, he decided to allow both his heronies to solve their problem according to this approved method which had won such applause for Chimène and Émilie. In *Rodogune*, the captive princess who gives her name to the piece stands in conflict between her love for the Prince Antiochus, and her duty, which requires her to demand the head of Cléopatre, the mother of Antiochus, for having murdered her betrothed. The complication of the situation is increased by the fact that the betrothed of Rodogune had previously been the husband of Cléopatre and as such the father of Antiochus. Accordingly Rodogune agrees to marry the young prince, if he will bring her the head of his mother:

> Votre gloire le veut, l'amour vous le prescrit
> . . . .
> *Pour gagner Rodogune il faut venger un père;*
> Je me donne à ce prix : osez me mériter,
>
> *Rodogune* 3 IV 1033—45.

Such are the revolting terms on which Rodogune agrees to bestow her hand. But we cannot blame her nor tremble for the fate of the queen Cléopàtre; for the latter has made precisely the same proposition to Antiochus concerning Rodogune, of whom she is jealous for having won away the affections of her husband. Corneille here introduces another complication by giving Antiochus a twin brother, Seleucus, The secret of priority of birth is known only to the mother. Who then shall succeed to the throne? Cléopatre sees her opportunity to take revenge on Rodogune. Summoning her two sons, she agrees, on her approaching abdication, to declare that one the elder who shall bring her the head of Rodogune:

> Si vous voulez régner, le trône est à ce prix,
> Entre deux fils que j'aime avec même tendresse,
> Embrasser ma querelle est le seul droit d'aînesse:

> *La mort de Rodogune* en nommera l'aîné.
> . . . .
> Je vous le dis encor, le trône est à ce prix;
>
> *Rodogune* 2 II 642—70.

In *Héraclius*, we find another captive princess in the person of Pulchérie. She seeks glorious revenge on the emperor, Phocas, for having murdered her father and cheated her out of her birthright. Like her predecessors, she defies the tyrant to his face with the bold threat:

> *je serai la conquête*
> *De quiconque à mes pieds apportera ta tête:*
>
> *Héraclius* 3 II 1047—48.

In *Andromède*, history gives way to mythology, but the heroine still belongs to the school of Corneille. Instead of being oppressed by a ruthless tyrant, like Pulchérie, she is threa-tened by a sea-monster to whom she is exposed on the rockbound coast. What is the moment in which we are compelled to recognize and admire the worth of this heroine? It is the moment when Cassiope, the proud mother of the princess, makes her daughter's hand the prize to the one who shall bring her the monster's head. To Phinée she says:

> Andromède est à toi si tu l'oses gagner.
>
> *Andromède* 3 II 916.

In *Don Sanche d'Aragon*, which is merely a heroic comedy, we do not look for the shedding of blood. But we do find the heroine, who makes her hand the reward to the one who shall bring her, not a bleeding head, but a ring which she has entrusted to the keeping of Carlos, the knight of obscure birth. Dona Isabelle would gladly bestow her hand upon this brave young courtier, but her duty compels her to make her hand the reward to the young scion of noble birth who shall get the ring away from Carlos. To her suitors, she says:

> Rivaux, ambitieux, faites-lui votre cour :
> Qui me rapportera l'anneau que je lui donne
> Recevra sur-le-champ ma main et ma couronne.
>
> *Don Sanche* 1 III 304—6.

Viewing Andromède and Dona Isabelle as slight digressions from the type of tragic heroines, we are greeted in 1652, by Eduïge, princess of Lombardy, who revives the system of Corneille once more. Incensed at Grimoald for having deserted her political cause, she agrees to marry the man, who shall murder the traitor. Proudly she proclaims :

> Et mes ardents souhaits de voir punir son change
> Assurent ma conquête à *quiconque me venge.*
> . . . .
> Pour gagner mon amour il faut servir ma haine :
> A ce prix est le sceptre, à ce prix une reine ;
>
> *Pertharite* 2 I 391—96.

With *Pertharite* we close the first period of Corneille. It remains to speak of a play which caused Corneille much solicitude. This play was *Nicomède*. The subject matter offered the poet full material for one of those tragedies in which he delighted, but he determined to deal with it in a new way. Instead of making revenge the mainspring of his drama, he resolved to see, what he could do with the sentiment of magnanimity, with which to arouse the spectator's admiration. Nevertheless, he was not over-confident. In his preface to the reader, he says : «Voici une pièce assez extraordinaire ; aussi est-ce la vingt et unième, que j'ai fait voir sur le théâtre ; et après y avoir fait réciter quarante mille vers, *il est bien malaisé de trouver quelque chose de nouveau, sans s'écarter un peu du grand chemin et se mettre au hasard de s'égarer*». Corneille was by this time too well trained by the public taste to care to attempt untried innovations in play writing, and this is why he apologizes for his experiment with *Nicomède*. According to the historical data, Prusias, king of Bithynia, excludes his own son, Nicomède, from the throne in favor of the son by a second wife, and he plots the assassination of Nicomède. The latter, becoming aware of the plot, with the support of faithful followers seizes the throne which is his birthright, and orders his tyrant father to be put to death.

Corneille finding this subject too gruesome, though we fail to see why it is any more revolting than his favorite tragedy of *Rodogune*, made various changes.

He does not represent the father and son as seeking to destroy each other. He depicts the king as being under the influence of his unscrupulous wife, Arsinoé, and Nicomède as a high-minded prince, who espouses the cause of Laodice, the persecuted queen of Armenia. The dénouement is a most unexpected *coup de théâtre*. The son of Arsinoé, Attale, recognizing the right of Nicomède to the throne, magnanimously refuses to become king.

If we consider the material out of which this play is built, we see at once all the elements of a tragedy of the old school. Taking previous works as a model, we should have every reason to expect that Laodice, persecuted by the tyrant Prusias and forced into a marriage alliance against her will, would demand that her lover Nicomède murder his own father, avenge his own wrongs according to history and win the hand of his lady by avenging her wrongs at the same time. That Corneille saw these possibilities is clear; for he tells us that in the construction of this drama, he purposely avoided the beaten track. The tragic element is wanting in *Nicomède*. Its place is supplied by the almost superhuman magnanimity of the leading characters.

According to the second method of revenge, the heroine of Corneille undertakes her revenge herself without the intervention of a third person. This method is first adopted by Cornélie. The widow of Pompey is a captive in the hands of Caesar. She aspires to become the wife of the author of her misfortunes for the purpose of killing him. She says to him:

> Heureuse en mes malheurs, si ce triste hyménée,
> Pour le bonheur de Rome, à César m'eût donnée,
> Et si j'eusse avec moi porté dans ta maison
> D'un astre envenimé l'invincible poison;
>
> *Pompée* 3 IV 1017—20.

And again:

> J'attends la liberté qu'ici tu m'as offerte,
> *Afin de l'employer toute entière à ta perte;*
>
> *Pompée* 4 IV 1377—78.

Such was Corneille's conception of the bereaved widow of Pompey. Mlle. Clairon, however, a distinguished actress of the last century at the Théâtre Français, found the Corneille heroine so repugnant that she refused to play the role. In her memoirs, she writes: «L'opinion publique fait de Cornélie un des beaux rôles du théâtre. Ayant à jouer ce rôle, j'ai fait sur lui toutes les études dont j'étais capable. Aucune ne m'a réussi. La modulation que je voulais établir d'après le personnage historique n'allait point du tout avec le personnage théâtral. Autant le premier me paraissait noble, simple, touchant, autant l'autre me paraissait gigantesque, déclamatoire et froid. Je me gardai bien de penser que Corneille et le public eussent tort, ma vanité n'allait point jusque-là; mais pour ne pas la compromettre, je me promis de me taire et de ne jamais jouer Cornélie. Après ma retraite les Commentaires sur Corneille et le Mot Esprit dans les Questions encyclopédiques par Voltaire ont paru; lisez-les: si je me suis trompée, l'exemple d'un si grand homme me consolera».

In the time of Corneille, however, Cornélie produced quite another impression. Saint Évremond admired her for the very reason that she did not obtrude her widow's woe, but sought revenge after the manner of a real tragic heroine. He says of her: «De toutes les veuves, qui ont jamais paru sur le théâtre je n'aime voir que la seule Cornélie, parce qu'au lieu de me faire imaginer des enfants sans père et une femme sans époux, ses sentiments tout romains rappellent dans mon esprit l'idée de l'ancienne Rome et du grand Pompée».[1]

Corneille himself could not have expressed himself better in regard to his ideal of a tragic heroine. Her threat of revenge did have the genuine tragic ring, and if this threat lent *éclat* to the character of Cornélie, why should it not produce the same effect with other heroines? Corneille resolved to try this device again and he accordingly allowed his Rodelinde in *Pertharité* to consent to a marriage with the tyrant Grimoald:

> Pour être à tous moments maîtresse de ta vie,
> Pour avoir l'accés libre à pousser ma fureur,
> Et mieux choisir la place à te percer le coeur.
> . . . .
> A ces conditions prends ma main, si tu l'oses
>
> *Pertharite* 3 III 996—1000.

Rodelinde was not a success, she was on the contrary a pronounced failure, the heroine of Corneille's most unfortunate tragedy. But Corneille remained undaunted. On his return to playwriting, he expressed his faith in his old methods by putting almost the identical words of Rodelinde into the mouth of a new heroine Viriate, whom Corneille describes as «une pure idée de mon esprit». She declares in her heroic moment, that in order to avenge the death of her lover, Sertorius, she will marry his murderer:

> Pour être à tous moments maîtresse de sa vie;
> Et je me resoudrois à cet excès d'honneur,
> Pour mieux choisir la place à lui percer le coeur.
> . . . .
> Et recevez enfin ma main, si vous l'osez.
>
> *Sertorius* 5 IV 1782—87.

Ildione, princess of Gaule, taking Viriate as model, decides to solve her problem in the same way. She determines

---

[1] Saint Évremond. Dissertation sur l'Alexandre de Racine.

to marry the tyrant Attila in order to murder him. To her lover, Ardarie, she lays bare her plan:

> *Et comme j'aurai lors sa vie entre mes mains,*
> Il a lieu de me craindre autant que je vous plains.
> *Assez d'autres tyrans ont péri par leurs femmes:*
> Cette gloire aisément touche les grandes âmes,
> Et de ce même coup qui brisera mes fers,
> Il est beau que ma main venge tout l'univers.
>
> Attila 2 VI 699—704.

This idea of marrying the tyrant in order to murder him, which apparently had such a great fascination for Corneille, was not in this instance, as we might be inclined to suppose, a mere repetition of a stroke which the poet had used with success in delineating previous heroines. — Ildione was no slavish imitator of Cornélie, Rodelinde and Viriate. In her tragic threat, she but follows the facts handed down in history by Ammianus Marcellinus, in his history of the Roman Empire, where it is recorded that Attila perished at the hand of his bride on his wedding night «Attila . . . noctu mulieris manu cultroque confoditur».[1] This idea had an irresistible charm for Corneille. Even when the heroine does not make the bloody threat herself, such an idea is suggested. In *Cinna* the hero depicts the state of anarchy at Rome by the graphic description:

> Le mari par sa femme en son lit égorgé ;
>
> Cinna 1 III 200.

Cléopatre also tries to poison the mind of her son Antiochus against his bride by imputing to her such an intention, at which Rodogune exclaims indignantly

> on m'impute un coup si plein d'horreur,
> *Pour me faire un passage à vous percer le coeur.*
>
> Rodogune 5 IV. 1761—62.

The wicked queen Arsinoé also makes the same insinuation

---

[1] See Marty-Laveaux. Oeuvres de Corneille. vol 7, notes on *Attila*.

against the high-minded Laodice. With a look full of treacherous meaning, she asks her son, the lover of Laodice:

> Pourras-tu dans son lit dormir en assurance?
> *Nicomède* 5 I 1500.

Thus we see that even the women who do not meditate revenge are imputed to do so, And likewise the women who have no cause for revenge resort to *raisonnements*, in order to make a glorious revenge possible. For example the plaintive Sabine, after having confessed to herself that the good of the State demands a mortal contest between Rome and Alba Longa, nevertheless deplores that two otherwise friendly peoples should be obliged to meet under those circumstances. She, therefore, begs either her husband or her brother to murder her in order that the other may have the glory of avenging her death. To them she therefore makes the following singular proposition:

> Qu'un de vous me tue, *et que l'autre me venge:*
> Alors votre combat n'aura plus rien d'étrange;
> *Horace* 2 VI 631—32.

In *Attila*, we find an echo, as it were, of Corneille's early days. The princess Honorie is being wooed by Valamir, king of the Ostrogoths. As if thinking of Cinna and evidently prepared to take the life of Attila as a last resort, if necessary, he asks her:

> N'est-ce que par le sang qu'on peut vous obtenir?

But Honorie, though apparently familiar with the conventional stipulation of the Corneille heroine, surprises us by replying:

> Non, je ne vous dis pas qu'*aux dépens de sa tête*
> Vous vous fassiez aimez, et payiez ma conquête.
> . . . .
> Régnez comme Attila, je vous préfère à lui;
> *Attila* 2 II 464—87.

Later in the play, however, Honorie does not disappoint us. Being degraded by Attila to marry a simple captain of the guard, she smarts under the indignity, but rises to the height of her sister heroines, by contemplating her humble suitor and reasoning:

> Ma gloire pourroit bien l'accépter sans scrupule,
> Tyran, et tu devrois du moins te souvenir
> Que s'il n'en est pas digne, il peut le devenir.
> . . . .
> *Ta vie est en mes mains, dès qu'il voudra me plaire,*
> *Attila* 4 III 1250—61.

«Vengeance!» was the cry of the Corneille heroine. How then could the poet bring his last tragedy more effectively to a close, than by allowing Palmis, the sister of Suréna, to exclaim, on hearing of the murder of her brother!

> Suspendez ces douleurs qui pressent de mourir,
> Grands Dieux! et dans les maux où vous m'avez plongée,
> *Ne souffrez point ma mort que je ne sois vengée!*
> *Suréna* 5 V 1736—38.

The cry of Palmis might well serve as the groundwork for a new tragedy of the Corneille pattern. It was eminently fitting that the theatre of Corneille should close with this tragic cry of vengeance on the high heroic plane where it began.

A person unacquainted with the theatre of Corneille would infer from the foregoing examples of heroines thirsting for revenge that the tragedies in question must be of an intensely violent and tragic nature. But such is not the case. In no instance is the heroine presented with a bloody head. Chimène pardons Rodrigue for the good of the State. Émilie becomes reconciled to Augustus. Rodogune does not compel Antiochus to bring her the head of Cléopatre. The lover of Pulchérie wins the hand of his bride without acceding to her murderous proposition. In like manner, we learn of no tyrant's being murdered in his bed at the hand of a bloodthirsty bride. Cornélie's last speech is a magnificent eulogy of the Caesar whom she was seeking to destroy. Rodelinde is prevented from carrying out her plan by the anti-climactic return of her husband. As to Viriate's threat that she will pierce Perpenna to the heart, we do not learn the outcome, the tragedy closing with a magnanimous reconciliation between Pompée and Aristie, to which Viriate lends her presence. Finally and most curious of all, Ildione, who, according to history, as we have shown, really did murder Attila on the night of her marriage to the famous Scourge of God, is not allowed in the play of Corneille to accomplish this purpose. Corneille explains his deviation from history, as follows «Il épousa Ildione . . . Il est constant qu'il mourut la première nuit de son mariage avec elle. Marcellin dit qu'elle le tua elle-même et je lui en ai voulu donner l'idée quoique sans effet».[1] Corneille seems therefore to have had an aversion for the actual accomplishment of the bloody threats, which he puts into the mouth of his heroines. Shakspeare would have gloried in carrying the threat out to the letter, and this is one reason why the Shakspearean tragedy is still considered barbarous in France. Corneille, in solving the problems of his heroines, was guided by a certain influence which pervaded the seventeenth century, the influence of Descartes. According to the Cartesian philosophy, generosity and magnanimity were made the highest virtues, and they were the very virtues with which Corneille endowed his heroines most strongly in the closing scenes of his dramas. The heroine's bloody threat he purposely averted «par un simple changement de volonté». Whatever she may threaten to do, she does not cause us any uneasiness for the hero or tyrant whose life is at stake. Like the «Kill Claudio!»[2] of Shakspeare's Beatrice, we realize that after all it is only a case of much ado about nothing. It is this very absence of real tragic interest, which detracts from the so-called tragedies of Corneille. Even in the time of Corneille this want was

---

[1] Attila. Au Lecteur.
[2] Much Ado about Nothing 4 I.

felt by the public, who refused to admire the tragedy of *Agésilas*. Corneille would seem in this work to have done his utmost to produce a tragedy which should be in the least possible degree tragic. He tells us «La manière dont je l'ai traitée n'a point d'exemple parmi nos français, ni dans ces précieux restes de l'antiquité qui sont venus à nous et c'est ce qui me l'a fait choisir . . . *On court à la vérité quelque risque de s'égarer et même on s'égare assez souvent quand on s'écarte du chemin battu ;* mais on ne s'égare pas toutes les fois qu'on s'en écarte : quelques-uns en arrivent plus tôt où ils prétendent et chacun peut hasarder à ses périls.»

The heroines of *Agésilas* illustrate the innocuous type of Corneille carried to the extreme. The plot of *Agésilas* may be briefly stated as follows :

Elpinice formerly betrothed to Cotys, now loves Spitridate
Aglatide   »   »   » Spitridate now loves Cotys
Mandane is beloved by Cotys and also by Agésilas.

Without going into the ingenious raisonnements which make up the play, it is enough to say that Elpinice marries Spitridate, Aglatide, Agésilas ; and Mandane, Cotys. Hémon calls *Agésilas* a vaudeville. He might also have called it a game of bézique.

In a word, the tragic heroines of Corneille, with but few exceptions, are not tragic. Jocaste and Sophonisbe, to be sure, die in accordance with historic and theatrical tradition, and the Eurydice of Suréna, a heroine who already shows the pathetic influence of Racine on the muse of Corneille, dies of grief at the hapless fate of the hero of the play. But in general we can say that of all the creations of Corneille, only one is really tragic, and that is the Cléopatre of *Rodogune*. She is genuinely, monstrously tragic. Determined at any cost to destroy her hated rival, Rodogune, she drinks of the poisoned cup, in order to reassure the princess, and thus induce her to drink after her. The deadly potion, however, contrary to her expectations, acts instantly, and the Queen Cléopatre dies in fearful agony, without having accomplished the destruction of Rodogune. The tragic fitfth act of *Rodogune* thus closes on a situation, than which Sardou could not devise a more thrilling. Corneille did after all possess the divine spark.

PART. II. OTHER REQUISITES WHICH GRADUALLY BECAME A FIXED PART OF CORNEILLE'S DRAMATIC SYSTEM.

1. Their «gloire».

In the foregoing chapters we have treated of those elements in the heroines of Corneille, which the poet himself discusses more or less fully for our enlightenment. We have found that he applied his theories consistently, as long as he continued to write for the theatre. The aristocratic heroine racked by conflicting emotions, burning with political ambition and thirsting for glorious revenge, became the ideal type which he introduced anew from play to play. She became a fixed part of his dramatic system. Did she gradually become monotonous? No, not from Corneille's point of view. From a seventeenth century stand point, she would have been called regular, and regularity was a sine qua non in the literary France of two hundred years ago.

In the following chapters we propose to show that this penchant for regularity influenced Corneille still more in the delineation of the minor details of his characters. There were certain elements, for which the poet had a great fondness, as especial marks of *bienséance*. As we read the first half dozen of Corneille's works we gradually see how they are made use of. As we read on, we, see them becoming more and more fixed in the poet's dramatic system, And towards the close of his career, they reappear with a persistency, which almost leads us to wonder whether Corneille did not write tragedies with his eyes shut. With the regularity of clockwork these elements would seem to introduce themselves, of their own accord, with little or no exertion on the part of the poet. In short they were as so many unconscious requisites to the art of the tragic poet.

First and foremost of these unconscious requisites is the omnipresence on the lips of the Corneille heroine of the word «gloire». Its pompous sonorousness is the keynote of the Corneille tragedy. No heroine can declaim at any great length without bringing the word in. It is her catchword *par excellence*, her final reply. According to Marty-Laveaux, the synonyms of the word are *éclat, splendeur, gloire celeste, fierté, orgueil en bonne ou en mauvaise part; gloire en parlant de la réputation des femmes, du sentiment qu'elles ont de leur honneur.*» If now we add to this list the meaning of politilical aggrandizement, it will be complete. We have seen sufficiently that the Corneille heroine finds her chief glory in politics.

As Chimène is the best known of Corneille's heroines, let us take her as a model in the use of the word «gloire». On hearing of the death of her father, she reflects at once:

Il y va de ma gloire, il faut que je me venge;
Le Cid 3 III 842.

And in the same language, she exhorts Rodrigue, going out to fight the duel for her hand:

En cet aveuglement ne perds pas la mémoire
Qu'ainsi de ta vie, *il y va de ta gloire,*
ibid 5 I 1505—6.

It is the same reflection which Irène makes thirty six years later, as she apprehends being jilted by her lover:

Après deux ans d'amour, *il y va de ma gloire*:
L'affront seroit trop grand, et la tache trop noire,
Pulchérie 4 II 1253—54.

Chimène states in a famous couplet the requirements which her duty places upon her in her relations with Rodrigue:

> Pour conserver *ma gloire* et finir mon ennui,
> Le poursuivre, le perdre et mourir après lui.
>
> *Le Cid* 3 III 847—48.

With that absolute fidelity to truth and justice, which characterizes the Corneille heroine, Chimène even praises Rodrigue for what he has done. Taking him, therefore, as a model of heroism, she says to him:

> Ta funeste valeur m'instruit par ta victoire;
> Elle a vengé ton père et soutenu *ta gloire*:
>
> . . . .
> Je suivrai ton exemple, et j'ai trop de courage
> Pour souffrir qu'avec toi *ma gloire* se partage.
>
> . . . .
> Et je veux que la voix de la plus noire envie
> Élève au ciel *ma gloire* et plaigne mes ennuis,
> Sachant que je t'adore et que je te poursuis.
>
> *ibid.* 3 IV 913—72.

In the next act Chimène appears with one of those apostrophes, so characteristic of the classic tragedy:

> Voile, crêpes, habits, lugubres ornements,
> . . . .
> Contre ma passion *soutenez bien ma gloire*;
>
> *ibid.* 4 I 1136—38.

On hearing that her lover has been killed she exclaims:

> Éclate, mon amour, tu n'as plus à craindre:
> . . . .
> Un même coup a mis *ma gloire* en sûreté,
>
> *ibid.* 5 V 1709—11.

We see how punctilious Chimène was in her reasoning on this, the day of her father's death. Instead of being overcome with grief at the terrible loss which she has sustained, she begins at once to argue pro and con the conflict in which she finds herself placed between her passion and her duty. Her first concern is to render satisfaction to her «gloire».

5

The subsequent heroines of Corneille are quite as mindful of their «gloire». It would require too much time, however, to take note of each and every instance in which they make mention of it, though it would be interesting to know how many times any given heroine makes use of the word in the course of a five act tragedy. We must, therefore, content ourselves with a limited number of quotations, which shall go to complete our conception of Corneille's ideal heroine.

Émilie analyzes the glory that will be hers, if her plot to murder Augustus succeeds:

> Joignons à la douceur de venger nos parents,
> *La gloire* qu'on remporte à punir des tyrans,
> . . . .
> Plus le péril est grand, plus doux en est le fruit;
> La vertu nous y jette, et *la gloire* le suit.
>
> *Cinna* 1 II 107—32.

It is a very similar idea which Pauline expresses to her former lover Sévère, as she spurs him on to rescue her husband. She says to him:

> Je sais que c'est beaucoup que ce que je demande;
> Mais plus l'effort est grand, plus *la gloire* en est grande.
>
> *Polyeucte* 4 V 1855—56.

Cléopatre, fearing that Caesar's infatuation for her may be only a fickle fancy, says:

> Mais je veux que *la gloire* anime ses ardeurs,
>
> *Pompée* 2 I 435.

Cornélie, after the death of her husband, debates with herself as to whether she has displayed sufficient grief:

> Je dois rougir pourtant, après un tel malheur,
> De n'avoir pu mourir d'un excès de douleur:
> Ma mort était *ma gloire*,
>
> *Pompée* 3 IV 999—1001.

Rodogune tersely makes it clear to Antiochus why he should bring her the head of his mother:

> *Votre gloire* le veut,
>
> *Rodogune* 3 IV 1033.

The wicked Cléopatre, planning the same method of destroying Rodogune, ponders and reflects:

> S'il étoit quelque voie, infâme ou légitime,
> Que m'enseignât *la gloire* . . . . . .
> *Rodogune* 2 II 471—72.

The wicked Arsinoé uses the word in a magnanimous compliment, which she pays her son:

> Vous êtes genereux, Attale, et je le voi,
> Même de vos rivaux *la gloire* vous est chère.
> *Nicomède* 3 VIII 1090—91.

Léontine declares openly

> Je punirai Phocas, je vengerai Maurice;
> . . . .
> J'en veux *toute la gloire*,
> *Héraclius* 2 II 493—95.

Andromède, piqued by the fact that the previous year twenty suitors had met their death in their vain efforts to rescue Nérée from the sea monster, says:

> Je vois d'un oeil jaloux *la gloire* de sa mort.
> *Andromède* 4 III 1287.

Donna Elvire describes her ideal heroes:

> Ils cherchent en tous lieux les dangers et *la gloire*,
> *Don Sanche* 1 I 78.

Donna Léonor, more skeptical, is inclined to doubt the disinterestedness of many heroes. For instance, after the exploits of a hero have won him a queen and a throne, she would like to know:

> S'en ira-t-il soudain aux climats étrangers
> Chercher tout de nouveau *la gloire* et les dangers?
> *Don Sanche* 1 I 87—88.

Donna Isabella is assured by Carlos:

> L'amour que j'ai pour vous est tout à *votre gloire:*
> *Don Sanche* 2 II 537.

The queen Laodice in her first interview with her lover, says:

> *Ma gloire* et mon amour peuvent bien peu sur moi,
> S'il faut votre présence à soutenir ma foi,
> > *Nicomède* 1 I 45—46.

And in the political tangle in which she finds herself ensnarled, Flaminius, the Roman ambassador, scouts the idea that she would lower herself by marrying Attale, He says:

> Cet hymen jetteroit un ombre sur *sa gloire*.
> > *Nicomède* 4 V 1451.

Prusias in despair appears before Arsinoé and declares to her that it is his intention to:

> Défendre *votre gloire*, ou *mourir à vos yeux*.
> > *Nicomède* 5 VIII.

Notice by the way that to die in presence of the beloved one was, also a favorite idea of the heroes of Corneille. Maxime[1] wished to die in the eyes of Emilie, and Sévère[2] in the eyes of Pauline. Eleven years after Nicomède, the aged Sertorius[3] expressed a wish to die at the feet of his adored Viriate, with whom, as he tells us, he was in love «par politique».[4]

Rodelinde, indignant at being compelled to marry the tyrant Grimoald, says:

> Après m'avoir fait perdre époux et diadème,
> C'est trop que d'attenter jusqu'à *ma gloire* même,
> > *Pertharite*. 1 II 215—16.
> Garde donc ta conquête, et me laisse *ma gloire*;
> Respecte d'un époux et l'ombre et la mémoire:
> > *ibid*. 2 V 718—20.

Rodelinde, however, finally agrees to marry the tyrant in

---

[1] Et souffrez que je meure aux yeux de ces amants.
> *Cinna* 5 III 1688.

[2] Je ne veux que là voir, soupirer et mourir.
> *Polyeuete* 2 I 436.

[3] Souffrez, après ce mot, que je meure à vos pieds.
> *Sertorius* 4 II 1256.

[4] Que c'est un sort cruel d'aimer par politique!
> *Sertorius* 1 III 370.

order to pierce him to the heart. But she makes such an agreement on condition that Grimoald murder her son before her eyes. She argues thus:

> Et consens à ce prix que ton amour m'obtienne,
> Puisqu'il souille *ta gloire* aussi bien que la mienne.
> *ibid.* 3 III 923-24.

On the unexpected return to life of the hero of the piece, Rodelinde vaunts the fidelity with which she as a widow has cherished his memory. She says to Pertharite.

> . . . .tout autre en ma place eût peut-être fait *gloire*
> De cet hommage entier de toute sa victoire . . .
> *ibid.* 4 V 1435-36.

Let us here digress once more to call the attention of the reader to Corneille's fondness for resurrecting his heroes. Emilie[1] and Pauline[2] are both startled by the re-appearance of former suitors, whom they had supposed to be dead.

On his return to the theatre in 1659, Corneille brought with him an original heroine, the political princess, Dircé. In the stirring scene which opens the play, she exhorts her lover

> Vivez pour faire vivre en tous lieux ma mémoire,
> Pour porter en tous lieux vos soupirs et *ma gloire*,
> *Oedipe* 1 I 81-82.

The passion of this heroine for her «gloire» is so great that she begins a monologue with the words:

> Impitoyable soif de *gloire*,
> *ibid.* 3 I 779.

and this thirst she decides to quench by dying for her country and thereby freeing Thebes from the pest. She declares:

> . . . Je fais *gloire* de mourir.
> *ibid.* 3 I 818.

---

[1] Mais je vous vois, Maxime, et *l'on vous faisoit mort!*
Cinna 4 V 1315.

[2] *Le bruit de votre mort* n'est point ce qui vous perd.
Polyeucte 2 II 464.

The two original heroines of *Sertorius* vie with each other in devotion to their «gloire». Aristie finally agrees to pardon her recreant husband, and makes him the following proposition:

> Si vous m'avez aimée, et qu'il vous en convienne,
> Vous mettrez *votre gloire* à me rendre la mienne;
> *Sertorius* 3 II 1113-14.

Her rival, Viriate, reminds Sertorius with a cold finesse:

> Et la part que tantôt vous aviez dans mon âme
> Fut un don de *ma gloire*, et non pas de ma flamme.
> *ibid.* 4 II 1285-86.

And this to the lover who had but declared that he would gladly die at her feet!

Imbued with the same ideal as Viriate, Sophonisbe spurns the amorous compliment which her husband sends to her from the battlefield, and coldly sends back word:

> . . . je le conjure, en cet illustre jour,
> De penser à *sa gloire* encor plus qu'à l'amour.
> *Sophonisbe* 1 I 33-34.

This quotation illustrates clearly what Corneille means when he says that the passion of love must content itself with second place in the drama.[1]

Sophonisbe also remonstrates on the same lines with her rival Éryxe, who is hopelessly in love with Massinisse:

> Si l'honneur vous est cher, cachez tout votre amour
> Et voyez à quel point *votre gloire* est flétrie
> D'aimer un ennemi de sa propre patrie.
> *ibid.* 1 III 202-4.

After agreeing to accept the hand of Massinisse on condition that she still be allowed to rule over her own territories, Sophonisbe reflects:

> Et c'est, pour peu qu'on aime, une extrême douceur
> De pouvoir accorder *sa gloire* avec son coeur;
> *ibid.* 2 V 709-10.

---

[1] Discours du poème dramatique.

> Je sais ce que je suis et ce que je dois faire,
> Et prends pour seul objet *ma gloire* à satisfaire.
>> *ibid.* 3 V 993-4.
> Quand il en sera temps je mourrai pour *ma gloire*.
>> *ibid.* 3 VI 1098.

Her last cry as she realizes the fall of Carthage is:

> Quelle bassesse d'âme! ô *ma gloire*, ô Carthage!
>> *ibid.* 5 I 1533.

We do not wonder that Corneille allowed his original queen Éryxe to exclaim on hearing of the death of Sophonisbe:

> Je la plains et l'admire:
> Une telle fierté méritoit un empire;
>> *ibid.* 5 VII 1803—4.

Camille, distrustful and jealous of the attentions which Othon is paying to her rival, says to her confidant:

> Peut-être, en ce moment qu'il m'est doux de te croire,
> De ses voeux à Plautine il assure *la gloire*:
>> *Othon* 3 I 837—38.

Aglatide queries as to the advantage which will accrue to her by marrying Cotys:

> Peut-être que mon choix satisferoit *ma gloire*.
>> *Agésilas* 4 IV 1571.

Mandane refuses Cotys out of political reasons, but consoles him by telling him:

> Non, seigneur, je vous aime;
> Mais je dois à mon frère, à *ma gloire*, à vous-même.
>> *ibid.* 4 V 1624—25.

Honorie declares to her lover:

> Pour peu que vous m'aimiez, Seigneur, vous devez croire
> Que rien ne m'est sensible à l'égal de *ma gloire*.
>> *Attila* 2 II 485—86.

Ildione, who, as we remember, marries Attila in order to murder him, explains her action as follows:

> Je l'épouserai donc, et réserve pour moi
> *La gloire* de répondre à ce que je me doi.
>> *ibid.* 2 VI 683—84.

The Bérénice of Racine leaves Rome heart-broken and in tears. In her final speech, she says:

> Adieu. Servons tous trois d'exemple à l'univers
> De l'amour la plus tendre et la plus amoureuse
> Dont il puisse garder l'histoire douleureuse.
> Tout est prêt. On m'attend. Ne suivez point mes pas
>   à Titus
> Pour la dernière fois, adieu, seigneur.
>   Antiochus.
>   Hélas!
>   *Bérénice* 5 VII.

Compare the simple pathos of her departure with the pomp with which Corneille's Bérénice returns to her Jewish dominions. On taking leave of the emperor, she says:

> Grâces au juste ciel, *ma gloire* en sûreté
> N'a plus à redouter aucune indignité.
> . . . .
> Rome a sauvé *ma gloire* en me donnant sa voix;
> . . . .
> Nous pourrions vivre heureux, mais avec moins *de gloire*
> . . . .
> Allons, Seigneur: *ma gloire* en croîtra de moitié
> Si je puis remporter chez moi son amitié.
>   *Tite et Bérénice* 5 V 1677—1770.

As a final example, let us quote the words of Pulchérie, the heroine whose coming, awakened such pleasurable anticipations in Mme. de Sévigné. In her first scene, she demonstrates clearly that she understands the ideals of Corneille. With admirable moderation and self control, she states her position to her lover:

> Je vous aime, Léon, et n'en fais point mystère:
> . . . .
> Ma passion pour vous, généreuse et solide,
> A la vertu pour âme et la raison pour guide,
> *La gloire* pour objet,
> . . . .
> L'amour entre deux coeurs ne veut que les unir;
> L'hyménée a de plus *leur gloire* à soutenir;
>   *Pulchérie* 1 I 1—80.

The *raisonnements* of Pulchérie at last drive Léon to despair and he cries out:

> Quelles illusions de *gloire* chimérique,
>
> *ibid.* 3 III 1005.

The foregoing quotations, in spite of their apparent prolixity, are by no means the only ones in which the heroines of Corneille dwell upon their «gloire». Indeed we have entirely, omitted to mention Sabine, Camille, the Infante, Médée, Livie, the Pulchérie of 1647, Plautine, Domitie and Eurydice, and these ladies by no means deviate from the high ideals, cherished by the heroines already quoted. One and all, they speak freely of their «gloire».

The casual reader, with the majestic verses of Corneille ringing in his ears might be inclined to attribute this striking frequency with which the word is used, to the necessity which Corneille was under of finding a suitable rhyme for words like *victoire*, *mémoire* etc. But an examination of one hundred and thirty-three quotations in which the word occurs, reveals the fact that the word occurs only forty-eight times in rhyme, nineteen times with *victoire*, fourteen times with *croire*, nine times with *mémoire*, twice with *histoire*, and once with *noire*. Corneille had not a large assortment of rhymes at his disposal it is true, and Malherbe was a hard task-master. Monotony in the rhyme was therefore unavoidable, or better expressed, the rhyme was monotonously regular. But we see that in the majority of cases, the word comes in the body of the line, thus showing that it was the idea contained in the word itself, more than the sonorousness of the rhyme which influenced Corneille in his lavish use of it.

Before leaving this point it is worth while to call attention to the way in which the Christian martyrs, Polyeucte and Théodore, employ the word. The wife of Polyeucte, seeing her husband, as he is being led away to execution, cries out in anguish:

> Où le conduisez-vous?

Félix

Polyeucte.

A la mort.

A *la gloire.*
Polyeucte 5 III 1679.

Théodore uses the word similarly. As if to rebuke those, who would force her into the conventional political marriage of the Corneille heroine, she says, as she makes a point:

. . *la gloire* où j'aspire est toute *une autre gloire,*
Théodore 2 IV 516.

To those who are inclined to see in the tragedies of «*Polyeucte*» and «*Théodore*», a sort of seventeenth century survival of the early religious dramas of the Middle Ages, we would call attention to a passage in the first French drama extant, the *Mystery of Adam*. After the creation of Eve, the Figura speaks to her of her duty as woman. Submission to her lord and master, Adam, is enjoined upon her. Celestial glory will be her reward. The Figura says:

Se tu li fais bone adjutoire
Jo te mettrai od lui en *gloire*
Mystère d'Adam. Edition Luzarche, Tours 1854.

√ Celestial glory, however, was not the concern of the Corneille heroine in general. Théodore was tabooed. A political heroine was more sympathetic to the public taste in the seventeenth century and especially to the admirers of the great Corneille.

Akin with the selfconsciousness of the Corneille heroine, which causes her never to forget her *gloire*, is her fondness for calling herself proudly by name. In the estimation of Voltaire, the finest line in the Cid is the one in which Chimene says to Rodrigue, as he goes out to the final duel

Sors vainqueur d'un combat dont *Chimène* est le prix.
Le Cid 5 I 1556.

That Corneille had great faith in the heroic powers of

this method of delineation is evidenced by the long line of heroines who follow the example of Chimene. For example:

Ce n'est point à *Camille* à t'en mésestimer:
Horace 1 III 249.

Commencez par *Sabine* à faire de vos vies
Un digne sacrifice à vos chères patries:
ibid. 2 VI 643—44.

La liberté de Rome est l'œuvre d'Émilie;
Cinna 1 II 110.

Sévère, connoissez *Pauline* tout entière..
Polyeucte 4 V 1335.

Souviens-toi seulement que je suis *Cornélie*.
Pompée 3 IV 1026.

Mais connois *Pulchérie* et cesse de prétendre.
Héraclius 1 II 142.

Mais gardez d'oublier qu' enfin je suis *Marcelle*,
Théodore 2 VI 672.

Vous leur immolez donc l'honneur de *Théodore*,
Théodore 3 I 752.

Je suis impératrice, et j'étois *Pulchérie*.
Pulchérie 3 I 754.

C'est par là seulement qu'on mérite *Eduige*.
Pertharite 2 I 495.

Quoi? *Dircé*, par sa mort deviendroit criminelle
Jusqu'à forcer Thésée à mourir après elle,
Oedipe 1 I 49—50.

Quoi? Jason, tu pourrois pour *Médée*
Étouffer de ta Grèce et l'amour et l'idée?
La Toison d'Or 2 II 876—77.

Sertorius, lui seul digne de *Viriate*,
Mérite que pour lui tout mon amour éclate.
Sertorius 2 I 389—90.

Sophonisbe, en un mot et captive et pleurante,
L'emporte sur *Eryxe* et reine et triomphante;
Sophonisbe 2 I 427—28.

Peut-être; mais, Seigneur, croyez vous *Bérénice*
D'un cœur à s'abaisser jusqu' à cet artifice . . .?
Tite et Bérénice 3 I 751—52.

This manner of allowing the heroine to speak for herself must have been regarded as a masterstroke of heroic character-drawing, as we shall see, if we examine the following incident. In the scene in «*Cinna*», in which Augustus discovers the conspiracy, the insignificant empress, Livie, appears on the boards with the following words:

>Vous ne connaissez pas encor tous les complices:
>Votre *Emilie* en est, Seigneur, et la voici.
>
>*Cinna* 5 II 1562—63.

As the rôle of Livie seemed superfluous to the actors, it met the fate of the Infante in the *Cid* and was gradually omitted altogether from the representation.[1] These lines were, therefore, put into the mouth of Émilie, who henceforth delivered them with all the bravado of a Corneille heroine.

We have given only a limited number of instances where the heroine calls herself by name. It was the habit of many of them to indulge in this practice repeatedly just as they did in sounding their «gloire». Chimène, Sabine, Emilie, Pauline, Cornélie, Pulchérie of 1647, Pulchérie of 1672 Viriate and Bérénice were by no means content to allow so effective a device to go unimproved. Their names had the genuine heroic ring; they also adapted themselves readily to the rhyme.

There is always a fascination in penetrating through the personages of any great author to the personality of the author himself. We have noticed the self-consciousness, the pompousness with which the heroines of Corneille assert themselves. Can we not see in them the influences of direct heredity? Do they not owe their character to the one who created them? How else are we to account for the absolute frankness with which Corneille praises his own literary efforts?

>Je sais ce que je vaux, et crois ce qu'on m'en dit![2]
>. . . . .

---

[1] In 1860 the rôle was permanently restored. See Marty-Laveaux vol. III p. 366.

[2] Compare *Sophonisbe* 3 V 993.
Je sais ce que je suis, et ce que je dois faire.

> Mon travail sans appui monte sur le théâtre :
> . . . .
> Je ne dois qu'à moi seul toute ma renommée
>
> *Excuse à Ariste* 36—41—50.

It was the character of the great Corneille which perpetuated itself in his tragic heroines. It was, therefore, eminently fitting that the last of the above lines should find a place upon the memorial tablet erected to Corneille in the court of the house in the Rue d'Argenteuil at Paris, where the great poet breathed his last.

---

2. Their pathetic element.

The second requisite with which Corneille as a matter of course invested his heroines was the pathetic element. A tragedy must be touching or it is no tragedy. The sufferings of the heroine must appeal to our sympathies. Thus it happens that Corneille allows his proud heroic women to shed tears when too sorely vexed by their problems, and to sigh when their political schemes fail to develop satisfactorily. This proneness to tears may also be regarded as a concession to the demand for «tendresse» on the part of the public. To the reader of the works of Corneille, the «*larmes*», «*pleurs*» and «*soupirs*» of his tragic heroines are as familiar as their cry of «*gloire*». Let us consider the pathetic element in the heroines of the four masterpieces and note as we go along to what extent Chimène, Camille, Sabine, Emilie and Pauline served as models for later heroines.

Chimène, in spite of her unrelenting pursuit of Rodrigue, is often in tears. Foreseeing the sad outcome of the quarrel between her lover and her father, she exclaims:

Honneur impitoyable à mes plus chers désirs,
Que tu vas coûter de pleurs et de soupirs! [1]

. . . .
Je sens couler des pleurs que je veux restenir; [2]

Le Cid 2 III 459—79

After the death of Chimène's father, the king is informed:

Chimène à vos genoux apporte sa douleur;
Elle vient tout en pleurs [3] vous demander justice.

ibid. 2 VII 636—37.

---

[1] Compare:
a) Cléopâtre in *La Mort de Pompée* 5 V 1789—90.
Ne vous offensez pas si cet heure de vos armes,
Qui me rend tant de biens, *me coûte un peu de larmes*,
b) Rodelinde to Eduïge in *Pertharite* 1 II 195—96.
Ce qui jusqu'à présent vous donne tant d'alarmes.
Sitôt qu'il me plaira, *vous coûtera des larmes;*
c) Eduïge addressed by Garibalde in *Pertharite* 2 I 403-4.
Grimoald inconstant n'a plus pour vous de charmes,
Mais Grimoald puni *vous coûteroit des larmes.*
d) Rodelinde greeted by *Pertharite* 3 IV 1009—10.
Oui, cet époux si cher à vos chastes désirs,
Qui vous a tant coûté de pleurs et de soupirs...
e) Plautine in *Othon* 5 III 1653—54.
Et son trépas pour vous n'aura pas tant de charmes,
Qu'à vos yeux comme aux miens *il n'en coûte des larmes.*

[2] Compare:
a) Camille in *Horace* 1 II 181.
Et combien de ruisseaux *coulèrent de mes yeux!*
b) Sabine in *Horace* 3 V 948.
Voyez couler nos pleurs sans y mêler vos larmes;
c) Pauline in *Polyeucte* 2 II 541.
Épargnez-moi des *pleurs qui coulent à ma honte;*
d) Créuse in *Médèe* 3 II 733—34.
Créuse en ses malheurs prend même quelque part.
Ses pleurs en ont coulé; Créon même en soupire,
e) Pertharité's description of the city of Milan, weeping at his misfortunes in *Pertharite* 5 V 1778
J'ai vu couler ses pleurs pour son prince impuissant;
f) Jocaste, as described by *Oedipe* 1 III 257.
J'en vis frémir son coeur, *j'en vis couler ses larmes;*

[3] Compare:
a) Aglante in *Andromède* 5 IV 1654.
Et *je viens toute en pleurs* vous en donner avis.
b) Ormène, announcing the death of *Surèna* 5 V 1711.
Elle vient toute en pleurs.

Chimène ends her sad narration to the king with the following words:

> *Mes pleurs et mes soupirs*[1] vous diront mieux le reste.
> ibid. 2 VIII 670.

In the next act the confidant Elvire informs us:

> Chimène est au palais, *de pleurs toute baignée,*[2]
> ibid. 3 I 765.

Don Sanche, the rival of Rodrigue, assures Chimène:

> Votre colère est juste, et *vos pleurs légitimes;*
> ibid. 3 II 774.

---

[1] Compare:
a) Massinisse interceding for Sophonisbe 4 III 1331.
   Mes pleurs et mes soupirs vous fléchiront-ils mieux?
b) Palmis in *Suréna* 3 III 1016
   Mes pleurs et mes soupirs rappelleront les siens,
c) the Infante, consoling Chimène. *Le Cid* 4 II 1144
   Je viens plutôt mêler *mes soupirs à tes pleurs*.
d) Achorée, relating to Cléopâtre the tragic death of *Pompée*. 2 II 495—96.
   ...... César même à de si grande malheurs
   Ne pourra refuser *des soupirs et des pleurs*.
e) Rodelinde in *Pertharite* 4 V 1409—10.
   N'attendez point de moi de *soupirs ni de pleurs:*
   Ce sont amusements de légères douleurs.
f) Pauline in *Polyeucte* 5 III 1606—7.
   Regarde au moins *ses pleurs*, écoute *ses soupirs;*
   Ne désespère pas une âme qui t'adore.
g) Andromède exposed upon the rocks. Timante begs the crowd of people assembled upon the shores, *Andromède*. 3 I 788.
   Avec respect *écoutons ses soupirs*;
h) Médée in *Médée* 1 I 15—16.
   Médée en son malheur en pourra faire autant:
   Qu'elle *soupire, pleure*, et me nomme inconstant;
i) Marcelle in *Théodore* 5 I 1529
   Marcelle n'attend plus que *son dernier soupir:*
j) Dircé, who describes herself, *Oedipe* 2 III 680 as:
   Ta véritable reine à *ses derniers soupirs*.
k) Pulchérie, describing the death of her mother in *Héraclius* 3 I 789.
   Elle mêla ces mots *à ses derniers soupirs*

[2] Compare:
   Stéphanie in *Théodore* 5 VII.
   Stéphanie entre ici, *de pleurs toute trempée*.

And he offers to avenge Chimène, the king being too remiss:

> Son cours lent et douteux fait *trop perdre de larmes*.[1]
>
> *ibid.* 3 II 785.

Chimène, *précieuse*, again rehearsing the sad death of her father with her confidant, thus apostrophizes her eyes:

> *Pleurez, pleurez*, mes yeux, et fondez vous en eau!
>
> *ibid.* 3 III 729.

The Infante comes to sympathize with Chimène with the following words:

> Je viens plutôt *mêler mes soupirs à tes pleurs*.[2]

---

[1] Compare:

a) Sabine in *Horace* 2 VII 691.
> Allons, ma soeur, allons, *ne perdons plus de larmes*:

b) Pauline addressed by her father. *Polyeucte* 3 IV 979—80.
> Employez mieux l'effort de vos justes douleurs:
> Malgré moi m'en toucher, *c'est perdre et temps et pleurs*;

c) Cléopâtre in *La Mort de Pompée* 4 V 1449—50.
> Ayez l'oeil sur le roi dans la chaleur des armes,
> Et conservez son sang *pour épargner mes larmes*.

d) Jocaste in *Oedipe* 3 II
> Et si votre vertu pouvoit croire mes larmes,
> Vous nous épargneriez cent mortelles alarmes.

e) Palmis in *Suréna* 5 IV 1683.
> J'ai perdu mes soupirs, ...

[2] Compare:

a) the *précieuse* language of Créuse, in the torments of death by poison. She says to her father, *Médée* 5 IV.
> Entre vos bras mourants permettez que je meure
> *Mes pleurs arrouseront vos mortels déplaisirs*;
> *Je mêlerai leurs eaux à vos brûlants soupirs*.

b) Sabine, beseeching her husband, *Horace* 4 VII.
> Pleurons dans la maison nos malheurs domestiques,
> . . . .
> *Mêle tes pleurs aux miens*.

c) Sophonisbe, receiving from Massinisse the final letter, Sophonisbe 5 I 1588.
> Qu'ont arrosé *ses pleurs*, qu'ont suivi *ses sanglots*.

To which Chimène replies:

> Madame: autre que moi n'a droit de *soupirer*.
> Le péril dont Rodrigue a su nous retirer,
> Et le salut public que vous rendent ses armes,
> A moi seule aujourd'hui souffrent encore *les larmes*:
> *ibid.* 4 II 1144—50.

At last Chimène finding her tears of no avail exclaims:

> Que pourraient contre lui *des larmes qu'on méprise*'.
> *ibid.* 4 V 1377.

In the last scene of the play, the Infante advises Chimène:

> Sèche tes pleurs, Chimène, et reçois sans tristesse [1]
> Ce généreux vainqueur des mains de ta princesse.
> *ibid.* 5 VII 1773—74.

And the king bids her:

> Prends un an, si tu veux, *pour essuyer tes larmes*
> *ibid.* 5 VII 1821.

Such is the manner in which Corneille developed the pathetic side of Chimène's character. It is quite natural, in view of the great success of Chimène, that Corneille should have laid stress on the pathetic side of his heroines, and not allowed them to waste all their energy in their striving for revenge and political glory. In *Horace*,[2] therefore, we find two women who vie with each other in tears. Their grief is justifiable, the one being threatened with the loss of her husband,

---

[1] Compare:
a) the words of Néarque to Polyeucte in regard to Pauline in *Polyeucte* 1 I 97-98.
   Votre retour pour elle en aura plus de charmes;
   Dans une heure au plus tard *vous essuierez ses larmes*;
b) the brusque words of Polyeucte to Pauline *ibid.* 2 IV 593.
   C'est trop verser de pleurs: *il est temps qu'ils tarissent*,
c) the King's command to Aglante in *Andromède* 5 IV 1659.
   Modérez vos frayeurs, et vous, *séchez vos larmes*.

[1] Compare:
   the *précieuse* language of Sabine, *Horace* 3 V 949—50.
   Enfin, pour toute grâce, *en de tels déplaisirs*,
   Gardez votre constance, et souffrez nos soupirs.

the other by that of her brother. The manner in which these two ladies express their grief hardly differs from that employed in the previous play. Their self-conciousness is ever perceptible, even when their grief is most poignant. Sabine, indeed, opens the play with a well-known verse, which prepares us for the calmness with which she discusses her sorrow later in the play:

> *Approuvez ma faiblesse, et souffrez ma douleur;*
> . . . .
> Le trouble de mon cœur ne peut rien sur mes *larmes*,
> *Horace* 1 I 1—8.

The affectation of this request on the part of Sabine that we be so kind as to pardon her tears, is continued by Camille, who in a moment of supreme grief, does not neglect like Chimène to couch her sorrow in exquisitely *précieuse* terms. Chimène had apostrophized her eyes and bade them melt away in tears. Camille, as she ponders over the catastrophe which threatens her, exclaims:

> Et combien de ruisseaux coulèrent de mes yeux!

Continuing her complaint, she soliloquizes farther in terms which the reader will readily recognize as among the most serviceable of all Corneille's methods of expressing grief:

> Et *quels pleurs j'ai versés* à chaque évènement,[1]
> *ibid.* 1 II 185.

---

[1] Compare:
a) Stratonice, sympathizing with Pauline in *Polyeucte* 2 III 573.
   Je vous ai plaints tous deux, *j'en verse encor des larmes;*
b) Pauline, addressed by her husband *Polyeucte* 2 IV 593.
   C'est trop verser de pleurs: il est temps qu'ils tarissent,
c) Emilie in *Cinna* 1 IV 302—4.
   Je verse assez de pleurs pour la mort de mon père;
   N'aigris point ma douleur par un nouveau tourment,
   Et ne me réduis point à pleurer mon amant.
d) Andromède chiding her lover, *Andromède* 4 III 1214—15.
   Vous avez donc pour moi daigné *verser des larmes*,
   Lorsque pour me défendre un autre a pris les armes!

Before the contest between Alba and Rome, Camille weeps again:

> *il faut bien que je pleure:*
> *ibid.* 2 V 572.

Her tears almost unman Curiace, who exclaims:

> *Que les pleurs d'une amante ont de puissants discours,*
> . . . .
> *N'attaquez plus ma gloire avec tant de douleurs,*
> *Et laissez-moi sauver ma vertu de vos pleurs;*
> . . . .
> *Allez, ne m'aimez plus, ne versez plus de larmes,*
> *ibid.* 2 V 577—87.

The old Horace finding both Camille and Sabine in tears, upbraids Horace and Curiace for allowing themselves to be affected by such feminine weakness. Scornfully he asks:

> *Prêts à verser du sang, regardez-vous des pleurs?*
> *Fuyez, et laissez-les déplorer leurs malheurs*
> *ibid.* 2 VII 681—82.

Sabine then recovers her self-possession and says to Camille:

> *Allons, ma soeur, allons, ne perdons plus de larmes*
> *ibid.* 2 VII 691.

---

e) Hypsipyle, as described by Jason in *Médée* 1 I 11—16.
   Elle jeta des cris, elle versa des pleurs.
   . . . .
   Médée en son malheur en pourra faire autant:
   Qu'elle soupire, pleure, et me nomme inconstant;
f) Flavie condoling with Plautine in *Othon* 5 VI 1795—96.
   Tout ce que peut l'effort de ce cher conquérant
   C'est de verser des pleurs sur Vinius mourant,
g) Dircé in *Oedipe* 5 VIII 1946.
   Seigneur, il n'est saison que de verser des larmes.
h) Rodelinde, bewailing the loss of her dominions. *Pertharite* 1 I 65—66.
   Et j'ai versé des pleurs, qui n'auroient pas coulé,
   Si votre Grimoald ne s'en fût point mêlé.;
i) Arsinoé, addressing Nicomède, in *Nicomède* 4 II 1281—82.
   Et sur votre tombeau mes premières douleurs
   Verseront tout ensemble et mon sang et mes pleurs.

The tears of the two women finally communicate themselves to the old Horace. Like Charlemagne and Roland in the mediaeval *Chanson de Roland*, he is moved to tears. As he takes leave of his son, who goes forth to mortal combat, he reflects:

> Moi-même en cet adieu *j'ai les larmes aux yeux*.
> *ibid.* 2 VIII 709.

Sabine complains that she and Camille are forbidden to witness the contest:

> Julie, on nous renferme, *on a peur de nos larmes;*
> *ibid.* 3 II 775.

Camille muses on the consolation of tears:

> Et tout l'allègement qu'il en faut espérer,
> C'est de *pleurer* plus tard ceux qu'il faudra *pleurer*.
> *ibid.* 3 III 837—38.

After the contest, Sabine comes once more in tears and beseeches her husband:

> *Pleurons* dans la maison nos malheurs domestiques,
> . . . .
> *Mêle tes pleurs aux miens*.
> *ibid.* 4 VII 1372—77.

On hearing of the arrival of the king, she comes still again:

> Sire, écoutez Sabine, et voyez dans son âme
> Les *douleurs* d'une cœur, et celles d'une femme,
> Qui toute désolée, à vos sacrés genoux.
> *Pleure* pour sa famille, et craint pour son époux.
> *ibid.* 5 III 1595—98.

Émilie would seem to have taken her cue from the heroines who have preceded her; for in spite of the spirit of vengeance with which she is imbued, she gives way to tears at about the same intervals as Chimène, Sabine and Camille. Reflecting on the possibility of Cinna's losing his life in the conspiracy against Augustus, she says:

> Un cœur est trop cruel quand il trouve des charmes
> Aux douceurs que corrompt *l'amertume des larmes;*

> Et l'on doit mettre au rang des plus cuisants malheurs
> La mort d'un ennemi *qui coûte tant de pleurs.*
> *Cinna* 1 I 37—40.

To Cinna she says:

> *Je verse assez de pleurs* pour la mort de mon père;
> N'aigris point *ma douleur* par un nouveau tourment,
> Et ne me réduis point *à pleurer mon amant.*
> *ibid.* 1 IV 302—4.

In the fourth act, foreseeing a successful outcome of her conspiracy, she tells us:

> Mon cœur est sans soupirs, *mes yeux n'ont point de larmes,*
> *ibid.* 4 IV 1270.

Hearing, however, that her plot has been unsuccessful she exclaims in an outburst of passion:

> Je vous entends, grands dieux, vos bontés que j'adore
> Ne peuvent consentir que je me déshonore;
> Et ne me permettant *soupirs, sanglots, ni pleurs,*
> Soutiennent ma vertu contre de tels malheurs.
> *ibid.* 4 IV 1297—1300.

Pauline in *Polyeucte* has every reason to weep. She represents a loving faithful wife, who trembles for the life of her husband. She is not an avenging fury like Emilie. Still we find her giving vent to her grief in much the same manner. In the first scene she does not appear but there are several descriptions of her, which prepare us for her coming. Polyeucte in conversation with Néarque, refers to her as:

> Pauline, sans raison *dans la douleur plongée,*
> . . . .
> Elle oppose ses *pleurs* au dessein que je fois,
> . . . .
> Je méprise sa crainte, et je cède à *ses larmes*
> *Polyeucte* 1 I 13—17.

Néarque, zealous in his endeavors to convert Polyeucte says:

> . . . Laissez pleurer Pauline.
> *ibid.* 1 I 65.

and as he continues, he becomes affected like the Old Horace in a pathetic moment:

> Je ne puis vous parler que *les larmes aux yeux.*
>
> *ibid.* 1 I 79.

and with Pauline again in mind, he asks:

> Comment en pourrez-vous surmonter les douleurs,
> Si vous ne pouvez pas résister à des *pleurs?*
>
> *ibid.* 1 I 83—84.

Néarque urges Polyeucte to come and be baptized without delay. He argues:

> Votre retour pour elle en aura plus de charmes;
> Dans une heure au plus tard *vous essuierez ses larmes;*
> Et l'heure de vous revoir lui semblera plus doux,
> Plus elle aura *pleuré* pour un si cher époux.
>
> *ibid.* 1 I 97—100.

The foregoing quotations have already placed us in the proper attitude towards Pauline, and we are not surprised when in her first meeting with her husband she beseeches him:

> *Donnez à mes soupirs* cette seule journée.
>
> *ibid.* 1 II 118.

And when he leaves her exclaiming:

> Adieu: *vos pleurs* sur moi prennent trop de puissance;
>
> *ibid.* 1 II 122.

Pauline cries after her fleeing husband:

> Va, *néglige mes pleurs.*
>
> *ibid.* 1 III 125.

It is not necessary to follow the pathetic element in Pauline any farther. Like her predecessors she is a heroine ever conscious of her tears. Indeed she makes the deliberate resolve to try the effect of her tears on her husband and her father; on the one to induce him to renounce his conversion, on the other to mitigate his wrath. To her confidant she announces her plan:

> Avant qu'abandonner mon âme à mes douleurs,
> Il me faut essayer la force de mes *pleurs:*
>
> *ibid.* 3 II 815—16.

It was the same resolve which Sabine had made in the previous play:

> Allons-y *par nos pleurs faire encore un effort.*
> *Horace* 4 VII 1401.

By the time Corneille finished his fourth masterpiece he had exhausted his grief-formulas, or to be more just to the great poet, he had collected a sufficient number of expressions of pathos to suit the demands of the French classic tragedy. Why should he take the trouble to devise other methods for the expression of grief on the part of his heroines? If Chimène, Sabine, and Emilie pleased the public with their «*pleurs*», «*larmes*» and «*soupirs*», why should not Eduïge, Éryxe and Pulchérie meet with an equal measure of success by the same means? The skeptical reader might again be inclined to attribute the pathos of Corneille's heroines to the exigencies of the versification. *Pleurs, douleurs, malheurs, vainqueurs; larmes, armes, alarmes, charmes; soupirs, désirs, déplaisirs.* The assortment of rhymes was not overabundant, to be sure. But here as in the case of «*gloire*», if we examine, we shall find that not the rhyme but the idea was of prime importance with Corneille. The woman in tears was a permanent figure in French tragedy. Voltaire even explains the tears of his own heroines as an especial mark of *bienséance*. When his tragedy of *Zaïre* was translated into English, he was shocked at the excessive emotion displayed by the English actress, who played the title rôle. On hearing that the Sultan loved her no longer, the English Zaïre threw herself upon the ground in an agony of Oriental despair. The French Zaïre on the other hand, merely shed a few gentle tears. The Sultan says to her:

> Zaïrè, vous pleurez,

and Voltaire assures us that these lines always produced a profound impression upon people of taste. They were practically the same lines which had lent distinction to the character of

Émilie in Corneille's *Cinna*. Filled with apprehension as to the fate which her lover may have met with in seeking to destroy Augustus, Émilie is similarly accosted by her confidant:

Vous en pleurez,

3 V 1069.

If we go back to the beginnings of French poetry, we find that many a mediaeval hero and heroine sought consolation in tears. A tinge of sadness pervades the poetry of the Middle Ages. The isolated life which the nobles led in old times in their stately chateaux was conducive to introspection. Out of sheer ennui have come many of the most characteristic gems of the old troubadour poetry. The laments of Beatrice, comtesse de Die [1], conscious of her fine courage and her personal charms, remind us of many of the heroines of Corneille. To such as would reproach the heroines of the classic French tragedy, the weakness which their tears would seem to betray, we would merely says that from the French standpoint, tears are not unbecoming in a tragic hero or heroine. In the *Chanson de Roland*, the heroes are repeatedly represented as being in tears. Charlemagne [2] and Roland [3] are easily moved to tears. The hundred thousand knights weep at the death of Roland:

Idunc *plurerent* cent milie chevalier

Chanson de Roland, 3870.

and the greatest of all French epic poems closes with the following line, familiar to every admirer of the *Chanson de Roland*, a description of Charlemagne:

Pluret des oilz, sa barbe blanche tiret

Chanson de Roland 4001.

The heroines of Corneille are, therefore, thoroughly national in their proneness to tears. But are they so strictly na-

---

[1] See Bartsch's chrestomathie Provençale. p. 69—70.
[2] See l. 1404, 2856, 2943. Gautier edition. Tours 1874.
[3] See l. 1853, 2022, 2217.

tional in the fondness which they display for arguing over the cause of their tears? At this point the ever present self-consciousness of the Corneille heroine makes itself felt. In the midst of her tears she listens to arguments, which remind us of those days long since past, when Corneille himself was a student of law. A few examples will make this point clear. Camille grieving over the doom, which threatens her lover, is reminded by her confidant that Sabine is far more to be pitied. The confidant reasons:

> Elle est pourtant plus à plaindre que vous:
> On peut changer d'amant, mais non changer d'époux.
>
> *Horace* 1 II 145—146.

After the death of Curiace, the old Horace reasons in much the same manner:

> En la mort d'un amant vou ne perdez qu'un homme
> Dont *la perte est aisée à réparer dans Rome;*
> . . . .
> Et ses *trois* frères morts par la main d'*un* époux
> Lui donneront des pleurs bien plus justes qu'à vous;
>
> *ibid.* 4 III 1179—86.

Sabine in like manner takes up the same *raisonnement*, and says:

> Je soupire comme elle, et déplore mes frères:
> Plus coupable en ce point contre tes dures lois,
> Qu'elle n'en pleurait qu'un, et que j'en pleure trois,
>
> *ibid.* 4 VII 1344—46.

The discussion as to which of two persons is the more to be pitied in a given situation had great attractions for Corneille. In *Andromède*, the lover and the father of the heroine debate over the question, which one has the greater cause for sorrow in the death of Andromède. The father argues:

> Votre perte n'est rien au prix de ma misère:
> Vous n'êtes qu'amoureux, Phinée, et je suis père.
> Il est d'autres objets dignes de votre foi;
> Mais il n'est point ailleurs d'autres filles pour moi.
>
> *Andromède* 2 IV 714—17.

With the same arguments Plautine is consoled at the supposed death of her lover Othon:

> Mais il est juste aussi de ne pas trop pleurer
> *Une perte facile et prête à réparer.*
>
> *Othon* 5 V 1695—96.

Palmis the sister of Suréna chides the princess Eurydice, because she does not weep at the danger which menaces Suréna. But she explains Eurydice's apparent indifference, as follows:

> Mais j'ai tort, et la perte est pour vous moins amère:
> *On recouvre un amant plus aisément qu'un frère;*
>
> *Suréna* 4 II 1109—10.

3. Their Self-Control and Dissimulation.

Akin with the heroine's propensity to tears is her power of self-control, by which she is able to restrain her tears at will. The selfconsciousness, which never deserts a lady born and bred in the highest society, also enables the heroines of Corneille to comport themselves with the elegant repose of manner, which characterized the ladies of the Hôtel Rambouillet. If perchance a heroine allowed herself to be carried away by a transport of passion at the failure of some political scheme, there was always some father, lover or confidant to repress her and quietly remind her that her conduct was not in keeping with her station as a lady of noble birth. To illustrate this point, let us still remain with the heroines of the four masterpieces, referring by way of comparison to later and less-known heroines, as occasion requires.

Chimène, for example, realizes the Corneille ideal when she says:

> Je sens couler des pleurs *que je veux retenir;*
> *Le Cid* 2 III 479.

Sabine, too, when in her opening complaint, she reflects:
> *Commander à ses pleurs* en cette extrémité,
> C'est montrer, pour le sexe, assez de fermeté.
> *Horace* 1 I 13—14.

Emilie, likewise, when in the impassioned moment in which she plots the murder of Augustus, she stops to apostrophize her feelings, with the words:
> Tout beau, ma passion, *deviens un peu moins forte;*
> *Cinna* 1 II 125.

The ideal is thus firmly established, and insisted upon many times in the course of the various dramas. Chimène, ashamed of the weakness which causes her to weep over her father's death, begs the king:
> *Excusez ma douleur,*
> *Le Cid* 2 VIII 668.

Pauline likewise apologizes for the emotion which she betrays, as she narrates the sad story of her separation from her lover:
> Il s'appeloit Sévère: *excusez les soupirs,*
> Qu' arrache encore un nom trop cher à mes désirs.
> *Polyeucte* 1 III 171—72.

Sophonisbe recovers promptly from the shock which she receives when Massinisse proposes to her that she desert her husband:
> De grâce, *excusez ma surprise.*
> *Sophonisbe* 2 IV 637.

Chimène is advised by the king:
> Prends du repos, ma fille, et *calme tes douleurs*
> *Le Cid* 2 VIII 739.

And again with Rodrigue in mind he says to her:
> *Calme cette douleur,* qui pour lui s'intéresse.
> . . . .
> Ma fille, *ces transports ont trop de violence.*
> *ibid.* 4 V 1349—85.

Chimène has previously been advised by her confidant:

> Modérez vos transports, voici venir l'Infante.
>
> *ibid.* 4 I 1142.

It is the same counsel which Sabine and Camille receive from their confidant:

> Modérez vos frayeurs;
>
> Horace 3 III 865.

The Infante is of all Corneille's heroines, the one whose selfconsciousness is most unmistakable. To her confidant she has made her complaint, that her exalted birth prevents forever the idea of her marrying Rodrigue. The confidant asks if she means to remain forever in her gloomy revery; to which the Infante replies with perfect composure:

> Non je veux seulement malgré mon déplaisir,
> Remettre mon visage un peu plus à loisir.

And then after a short soliloquy, she stops short and says:

> Mais je tarde un peu trop: allons trouver Chimène,
>
> Le Cid 1 II 139—49.

Camille controls her passions well until after the death of her lover, when, as she reasons, there is no object in restraining them any longer:

> Eclatez, mes douleurs: à quoi bon vous contraindre?
>
> Horace 4 IV 1243.

The young Horace is especially stern towards weeping women. He bids his father:

> Mon père, retenez des femmes qui s'emportent,
>
> *ibid.* 2 VIII 695.

Even after the death of his sister, he reproves his wife severely:

> Sèche tes pleurs, Sabine, ou les cache à ma vue:
> . . . .
> Adieu: ne me suis point, ou retiens tes soupirs.
>
> *ibid.* 4 VII 1348—97.

Finally king Tullius pronounces the words which show

Sabine her duty as a heroic woman, as a heroine of the great Corneille:

> Sabine, écoutez moins la douleur qui vous presse;
> Chassez de ce grand cœur *ces marques de foiblesse*:
> C'est en séchant vos pleurs que vous vous montrerez
> La véritable sœur de ceux que vous pleurez.
> *Horace* 5 III 1767—70.

Emilie, therefore, on the recommendation of king Tullius, it would seem, for her solicitude concerning Cinna apologizes with the words:

> Pardonnez à mon amour *cette indigne foiblesse*.
> *Cinna* 1 IV 325.

The necessity of self-control shows itself in every tragedy of Corneille. If we compare his first heroine with his last, and his last with anyone of the women created by him midway in his career, we shall find this element predominant side by side with the pathetic element to which it forms a sort of complement. And in this point, be it said, Corneille showed unwonted variety in his poetic language, not relying always on the same formula of speech in similar situations. For example Médée is counselled in the following words:

> *Modérez les bouillons de cette violence*,
> Et laissez déguiser vos douleurs au silence.
> *Médée* 1 V 281—82.

Marcelle receives following advice:

> Madame, écoutez moins *des transports si bouillants*:
> *Théodore* 5 VI 1710.

and the immoderate emotion of Eduïge is subdued by the injunction:

> *Dissimulez* du moins *ce violent courroux:*
> *Pertharite* I IV 385.

In many instances, nevertheless, Corneille showed his profound faith in the utility of tried methods. His original heroine Viriate, for example, on being informed of the death of Sertorius, on whom she had staked her political hopes, says with an iron firmness to her rival:

> Madame, après sa perte, et parmi ces alarmes,
> *N'attendez point de moi de soupirs ni de larmes;*
> *Ce sont amusements* que dédaigne aisément
> Le prompt et noble orgueil d'un vif ressentiment:
> Qui pleure l'affoiblit, qui soupire l'exhale.
>
> *Sertorius* 5 III 1681—84.

Viriate was thoroughly *cornélienne*, though not entirely original. Ten years before, if we care to look back, we find Rodelinde expressing the same sentiments, on apprehending the death of Pertharite:

> *N'attendez point de moi de soupirs ni de pleurs:*
> *Ce sont amusements* de légères douleurs.
>
> *Pertharite* 4 V 1409—10.

In a similar manner the idyllic Andromède in 1650 holds herself up to her lover as a model of self-control in the following words:

> J'étouffe ma douleur pour n'aigrir pas la vôtre;
> Je retiens mes soupirs de peur de vous fâcher,
> *Et me montre insensible afin de moins toucher.*
>
> *Andromède* 2 III 647—49.

It is precisely the course which Plautine adopts towards her lover fourteen years later, and in much the same language:

> Tout ce que vous sentez, je le sens dans mon âme;
> J'ai mêmes déplaisirs, comme j'ai même flamme;
> J'ai même désespoirs; mais je sais les cacher,
> *Et paroître insensible afin de moins toucher.*
>
> *Othon* 1 IV 345—48.

The affinity which one heroine has for another is shown by still another example. Émilie in 1639 appears upon the scene with an apostrophe to her emotions beginning:

> Impatients désirs d'une illustre vengeance
> . . . .
> Enfants impétueux de mon ressentiment,
> . . . .
> *Vous prenez sur mon âme un trop puissant empire:*
> Durant quelques moments, souffrez que je respire,
>
> *Cinna* 1 I 1—6.

Thirty-five years later, Eurydice similarly apostrophizes her overzealous love for Suréna:

> *Amour, prends sur ma vertu un peu moins d'empire!*
> *Suréna* 1 II 238.

The instances which we have cited above, suffice to show the importance of self-control as a requisite to the Corneille heroine. Without following any definite plan, we have in this chapter chosen at random the heroines of the following years: 1635, 1639, 1650, 1662, 1664, 1674, thus covering the whole career of Corneille as tragic poet. If we had compared the same number of heroines taken from the tragedies of other years, the result would not have been far different. A heroine of tragedy must, in the estimation of Corneille, comport herself with studied moderation; or in the words of Honorie, a heroine of the year 1667:

> . . . il vaut mieux faire effort sur moi-même.
> *Attila* 2 I 449.

The same self-consciousness which enables the Corneille heroine to restrain her tears, would also seem to guide her in her use and abuse of her fondness for argument. The captive princess, seeking glorious revenge, is ever ready to enter into conversation on any subject which will allow her to make good points with her audience. But she seems to have the instinct, after a time, of having talked long enough. She seems to feel with Corneille that a tragedy has a fixed limit, and must come to an end. Voltaire says that the great public paid their five sous for two hours worth of recitation. Corneille took pains accordingly not to let his plays go beyond eighteen hundred lines. That seemed to him the suitable length. His heroines were, therefore, obliged to yield the stage to the other actors, after holding it a just amount of time. After the quarrel over the *Cid*, Corneille found himself more than ever obliged to bring the action of his plays within twenty four hours, and he, therefore, made use of a set of phrases, which should apprise the spectator that the action of the play was making suitable progress. Even before the *Cid* we find Médée, anxious to hear the effect of the poisoned robe on Créuse, interrupting the herald in his narration with the words:

Dépêche, ou ces longueurs attireront ma haine.

Medée 5 I 1298.

About to murder her children she says:

N'en délibérons plus, mon bras en résoudra.
Je vous perds, mes enfants; mais Jason vous perdra;

ibid. 5 II 1355—56.

The four masterpieces furnish us with fewer examples on the part of the heroines to hasten the action. The reason is that in his earlyt ragedies, Corneille was handling simpler subjects. The action spent itself easily in the five acts.[1] There was no need of the actors becoming impatient.

For comparison's sake, in order to make this point clear, let us consider again those heroines who have just distinguished themselves by their self-control. We shall find that, whatever the situation, they did not propose to waste time.

Eurydice brings her discussion as to coolness of her love for Pacorus, to a close by saying:

J'en dis trop; il est temps que je finisse.

Suréna 2 II 581.

The two original heroines of 1662 resemble her. Aristie in parley with her faithless husband, is undecided whether or not to return to his side. After both parties have sufficiently debated over the matter, she says:

---

[1] Compare:
a) Chimène addressed by her confidant. *Le Cid* 4 I.
   Modérez ces transports, *voici venir l'Infante.*
b) Pauline checking the condolences of her confidant. *Polyeucte* 1 III 264.
   Tais-toi, *mon père vient.*
c) Théodore closing her first scene with Cléobale in *Théodore* 2 II 444.
   Quittons ce discours, *je vois venir Marcelle.*

>Mais *il est temps qu'un mot termine ces débats.*
>
>*Sertorius* 3 II 1115.

Viriate brings her first long interview with her confidant to a close with the following words:

>Mais *nous en parlerons encore quelque autre fois:*
>Je l'aperçois, qui vient.
>
>*Sertorius* 2 I 472—73.

And thus she affords Sertorius the opportunity to make his entrance, a familiar device of Corneille. Here again, we find the original queen Viriate terminating her scene in the same manner as the Persée of *Andromède* twelve years before. Persée closes a discussion on the subject of Andromède's beauty with the proposition:

>*Mais nous en parlerons encore quelque autre fois.*
>*Voici le Roi qui vient.*
>
>*Andromède* 1 IV 251—52.

And the king is by this means introduced upon the scene. Corneille evidently thought well of this method of linking his scenes together, as he uses it in *Rodogune*, where Laonice yields the stage to the hero, by postponing her narration, as follows:

>*Je vous achèverai le reste une autre fois,*
>*Un des princes survient.*
>
>*Rodogune* 1 I 70—71.

Was it judicious on the part of Corneille to call the attention of his public to the fact that the discourses of his heroes and heroines were monotonous? Perhaps he became weary himself of the very methods which belonged to his dramatic system. In any case he certainly allows his characters not only to become impatient at the *longueur* of the speeches which they are obliged to listen to, but to express their ennui with unmistakable clearness. Pauline and Othon, discussing the unhappy lot which is theirs, the sacrifice which each must make in renouncing the other, are advised by the father of the lady:

> *Sans discourir* faites ce qu'il faut faire;
> *Othon* 4 I 1278.

It was the same advice which Rodrigue had given to Chimène. He begs her to strike him down with the words:

> *sans plus discourir,*
> Sauve ta renommée en me faisant mourir.
> *Le Cid* 3 IV 967—68.

Sophonisbe, disposed to discuss at length the propriety of her deserting one husband in order to marry another, is reminded by Massinisse:

> Quand *le temps est trop cher pour le perdre en paroles,*
> Toutes ces vérités sont des discours frivoles:
> *Sophonisbe* 2 IV 659—60.

Camille would seem to voice the sentiments of many another heroine when she bids her rival Plautine:

> Brisons là: *ce discours deviendroit ennuyeux.*
> *Othon* 4 IV 1407.

And finally the ferocious tyrant, Grimoald, puts an end to the importunities of his antagonist by declaring:

> Ah! c'est m'assassiner *d'un discours inutile:*
> *Pertharite* 2 IV 596.

Corneille, as we have seen, had a sufficient variety of expressions for hastening the action of his dramas.[1] «*Sans*

---

[1] Compare further:
a) Sabine in *Horace* 2 VII 691.
   Allons, ma soeur, allons, ne *perdons plus de larmes:*
b) Jason taking leave of Médée, *Médée* 2 IV 605—6.
   Mais, *sans plus de discours,* d'une maison voisine
   Je vais prendre le temps que sortira Nérine.
c) Créuse addressed by Jason, *Médée* 5 V 1509.
   Ne perdons point de temps,
d) Dircé addressed by Thesée *Oedipe* 1 I 97.
   Mais ne contestons point et sauvons l'un et l'autre:
e) Jocaste in *Oedipe* 4 II 1362.
   Qu'il vienne; *il tarde trop, cette lenteur me tue;*
f) Thamire in *Sertorius* 4 I 1207.
   N'y perdez point de temps, et ne négligez rien.

plus discourir», «*sans plus de discours*», «*sans discourir*», «*un discours inutile*», «*debats superflus*», «*ne perdons point de temps*», «*à parler sans fard*», «*sans plus tarder*», were among the most serviceable of his literary tools as a play-wright. At the same time they were fully in keeping with that self consciousness, which is a distinguishing trait of his tragic heroines.

---

4. Their polite breeding.

The same self-consciousness which enables the heroines of Corneille to keep their *gloire* ever in mind, to analyze the cause of their tears, and to refrain from all undue emotion, also furnishes them with that grace of bearing so essential to ladies in high society. With the Marquise de Rambouillet and her coterie ever before them as models, they could not help reflecting the etiquette of the Blue Chamber and other salons of Paris. In the heroines of Corneille, we therefore

---

g) Marcelle in *Théodore* 1 IV 384.
  Allez-y, Stéphanie, *allez sans plus tarder*.
h) Cassiope, addressed by Persée in Andromède 1 IV 442.
  C'est trop perdre de temps, courons à votre joie.
i) Cassiope in *Andromède* 5 III 1616.
  Un amant qui perd tout peut perdre des paroles;
j) Eduïge in *Pertharite* 4 II 1293.
  Tu perds temps; je n'écoute plus rien,
k) Sophonisbe in *Sophonisbe* 2 IV 702.
  Ne perdez point, Seigneur, *ces précieux moments*;
l) Sophonisbe in *Sophonisbe* 2 V 763.
  Allons, sans perdre temps,
m) Sophonisbe as described by Massinisse, *Sophonisbe* 3 I 789—90.
  Cependant cours au temple, et presse un peu la Reine
  D'y terminer des voeux dont *la longueur me gêne;*
n) Palmis, addressed by Orode in *Suréna* 3 III 1049.
  N'en parlons plus, Madame;

behold, not only a series of captive princesses seeking glorious revenge for wrongs suffered, but a bevy of society ladies, the *grandes dames* of the seventeenth century.

Chimène charmed all Paris by her refinement of manner. Hearing that her father and her lover are at swords points, the young girl has every reason to be agitated. We could easily pardon her, if she completely forgot the conventions of society at such a moment, but this aristocratic heroine does not forget to take leave in a ladylike manner of the Infante, with whom she has been in conversation:

    Madame, *pardonnez* à cette promptitude.
                                              Le Cid 2 IV 505.

The king having condoled with Chimène, after the death of her father and having promised to be a father to her, she is not at a loss to acknowledge his kindness:

    Sire, *de trop d'honneur* ma misère est suivie.
                                              ibid. 2 VIII 673.

We see in these two quotations the elegance and high-breeding of a woman of the world. Later in the play the manners of Chimène offer several examples of pleasing prudery, — pleasing at a time when the stage had only recently been rescued from a state of gross licentiousness. The modesty of Chimène met with the unstinted approval of the Hôtel Rambouillet. Her solicitude as to her reputation stamped her as a person of propriety. It is a thrilling moment, when Rodrigue comes to his betrothed, and begs her to kill him in such gallant terms:

    Assurez vous l'honneur de m'empêcher de vivre.
                                              ibid. 3 IV 850.

At such a moment nothing less than great presence of mind and a fine sense of propriety could enable the young girl to reply:

    Dans l'ombre de la nuit *cache bien ton départ:*
    Si l'on te voit sortir *mon honneur court hasard.*

> La seul occasion qu'aura la médisance,
> C'est de savoir qu'ici j'ai souffert ta présence :
> Ne lui donne point lieu *d'attaquer ma vertu.*
>
> *ibid.* 3 IV 975—79.

And again in the last act, when Rodrigue comes to take leave of her, she exclaims:

> Quoi! Rodrigue, en plein jour! d'où te vient cette audace?
> Va, *tu me perds l'honneur;* retire-toi, de grâce.
>
> *ibid.* 5 I 1465—66.

And as Rodrigue goes out to fight the final duel, she cries after him:

> Sors vainqueur d'un combat. dont Chimène est le prix.
> Adieu: *ce mot lâché me fait rougir de honte.*
>
> *ibid.* 5 I 1556—57.

In *Horace*, it is Sabine who represents the well bred woman. Camille, unable to bear the death of her lover with the equanimity worthy of a Corneille heroine, curses her fatherland and meets with a tragic death in consequence at the hands of her brother. Her grief was not without reason, but however natural we may find her woman's frenzy at such a time, it is clear that from the standpoint of the Hôtel Rambouillet, the demeanor of Sabine was far more pleasing. Moderation and extreme politeness characterize her every speech. She begins the play, as we have already pointed out with the apology:

> *Approuvez* ma foiblesse, et *souffrez* ma douleur;
>
> *Horace* 1 I 1.

She apologizes for the love which she bears her brother:

> Mais *excusez* l'ardeur d'une amour fraternelle;
>
> *ibid.* 1 I 115.

She chides her sister-in-law with much delicacy:

> Parmi nos déplaisirs *souffrez* que je vous blâme:
>
> *ibid.* 3 IV. 871.

And she begs the old Horace:

> Enfin, pour toute grâce, en de tels déplaisirs,
> Gardez votre constance, et *souffrez* nos soupirs.
>
> *ibid.* 3 V 949—50.

An example of the polite mingled with the sentimental is the symmetrical refrain with which Sévère and Pauline take leave of each other:

> Sévère
> Adieux, *trop* vertueux objet, et *trop* charmant.
> Pauline
> Adieu, *trop* malheureux et *trop* parfait amant.
> *Polyeucte* 2 II 571—72.

The confidant of Cléopatre, after the submission of Ptolomée to Caesar, describes her mistress as follows:

> Cléopatre s'enferme en son appartement,
> Et sans s'en émouvoir *attend son compliment*.
> *Pompée* 3 I 723—24.

It is the same mark of gallantry which Othon shows to the princess Camille, twenty three years later:

> Othon à la Princesse *a fait un compliment*,
> Plus en homme de cour qu'en véritable amant.
> *Othon* 2 I 399—400.

Othon makes love to Plautine in deferential terms:

> Madame, encore un coup, *souffrez que je vous aime*.
> *Othon* 2 II 541—42.

This quotation takes us back nineteen years to the occasion when the wicked Marcelle says to Théodore:

> Et si vous vous aimez, *souffrez que je vous aime*.
> *Théodore* 2 IV 492.

In the gallant speech of Sertorius to Viriate, we witness an excess of politeness on the part of the old general. As Viriate pronounces the word «love» Sertorius says:

> *Souffrez*, après ce mot, *que je meure à vos pieds*.
> *Sertorius* 4 II 1256.

Corneille's original heroine, Éryxe, takes leave of Sophonisbe with perfect consciousness of her own high breeding. She retires saying:

> Mais le Roi vient: adieu, je n'ai pas l'imprudence
> De m'offrir pour troisième à votre conférence,
> *Sophonisbe* 1 III 243—44.

An instance of faultless deportment is seen in the graceful manner in which Andromède, rescued from the sea-monster, acknowledges her indebtedness to her deliverer. To him she says:

> *Pardonnez*, grand héros, si mon étonnement
> N'a pas la liberté d'aucun remercîment.
>
> *Andromède* 3 III 972—73

As a final example of the gallantry with which the heroine was treated, let us regard Suréna in presence of Eurydice. Driven to despair because he is prevented from marrying her, he wishes to die and sacrifice his life to the memory of his beloved. He says to her:

> *Pardonnez* à l'amour, qui vous la sacrifie,
> Et *souffrez* qu'un soupir exhale à vos genoux,
> Pour ma dernière joie, une âme toute à vous.
>
> *Suréna* 1 III 254—56.

We have noticed that Corneille availed himself of a limited number of expressions to avoid wasting time. In the present chapter we have likewise observed the frequent recurrence of a select number of polite formulas, with which he seasoned the tone of the conversation of his characters. «*Pardonnez*» «*souffrez*» «*excusez*» «*de grâce*» «*de toute grâce*», — the number was adequate to establish the high breeding of his heroes and heroines, and make them congenial to the cultivated public of the seventeenth century.

Corneille also adopted another means of making his heroines sympathetic to the persons before whom they played. He invested them with hypercritical nicety in their language as in their manners. Affectation was really very far from being a characteristic of Corneille himself. On the contrary he conceived his tragedies in a bold spirit; his personages are conspicuous for the vigor and ruggedness of their character. But the atmosphere of Paris was infectious. With the establishment of the Hôtel Rambouillet, the *précieuses* began to make their influence felt. As far back as 1621, a lovesick prince in the «*Silvie*» of Mairet had charmed the public by the pretty way in which he spoke of his heart as the place:

<blockquote>Où l'amour avait fait son plus beau cabinet.</blockquote>

This is one of the first appearances in the French tragedy of that peculiar affectation in language, which was borrowed from Spain and Italy and carried to perfection by the deft litterateurs of the seventeenth century in France. It required a Molière and a masterpiece like *Les Précieuses Ridicules* to show up the folly of this habit in its true light. In Corneille,[1] the *précieuse* character of the women is most noticeable in their tendency to reflect on their sufferings and at the same time to express these sufferings in moderate terms. Chimène, in telling of the sufferings which the death of her father has caused her, speaks of «mon cœur outré d'ennuis» (Le *Cid* 2 II 448) and of the anguish of her heart as a «juste déplaisir». Sabine likewise refers to her solicitude for her husband and her fatherland as «les déplaisirs d'une âme» (*Horace* 1 I 11), and like Chimène speaks of «mon cœur accablé de mille déplaisirs» (1 I 132) Émilie in her entrance monologue constitutes her passions into a little family as Voltaire describes it, by addressing them in the following terms

<blockquote>
Impatients désirs d'une illustre vengeance
Dont la mort de mon père a formé la naissance,
Enfants impétueux de mon ressentiment,
Que ma douleur séduite embrasse aveuglément,
Vous prenez sur mon âme un trop puissant empire :
Durant quelques moments souffrez que je respire,
Cinna 1 I 1—6.
</blockquote>

The favor with which Émilie was received undoubtedly influenced Corneille in allowing Aristie, twenty-three years later to shine by a similar burst of *esprit*. But by this time, Corneille had become so mechanical in his literary methods

---

[1] See Rudershausen. Pretiöse Charaktere und Wendungen in Corneilles Tragödien. Mainz 1894.

that he introduced a curious symmetry into the speech of Aristie. The scene is so characteristic of the cold calmness of the poet in his later period, that we think it worthy to be quoted in full. Aristie is on the point of forgiving her recreant husband and returning to his side. She makes her position clear to him in the following compactly constructed lines :

> *Sortez de mon esprit, ressentiments jaloux;*
> *Noirs enfants du dépit*, ennemis de ma gloire,
> Tristes ressentiments, je ne veux plus vous croire.
> Quoiqu'on m'ait fait d'outrage, il ne m'en souvient plus.
> Plus de nouvel hymen, plus de Sertorius;
> Je suis au grand Pompée; et puis qu'il m'aime encore,
> Puisqu'il me rend son coeur, de nouveau je l'adore:
> Plus de Sertorius. Mais, Seigneur, répondez;
> Faites parler ce coeur qu'enfin vous me rendez.
> Plus de Sertorius. Hélas! quoi que je dis
> Vous ne me dites point, Seigneur: «Plus d'Emilie».
> *Rentrez dans mon esprit, jaloux ressentiments,*
> *Fiers enfants de l'honneur*, nobles emportements;
> C'est vous que je veux croire; et Pompée infidèle
> Ne sauroit plus souffrir que ma haine chancelle:
> Il l'affermit pour moi. Venez, Sertorius;
> Il me rend toute à vous par ce muet refus.
> Donnons ce grand temoin à ce grand hyménée;
> Son âme, toute ailleurs, n'en sera point gênée:
> Il le verra sans peine, et cette dureté
> Passera chez Sylla pour magnanimité.
>
> *Sertorius* 3 II 1012—32.

The tendency to introspection and to periphrastic analysis of the emotions on the part of Corneille's heroines is to be ascribed to the influence of the précieuses. His tragedies teem with *précieuses* situations and characters.

The Hôtel Rambouillet was the cradle of the *précieuses*, It was further a school of *bienséance* for Corneille in the delineation of his heroines. It was highly desirable that they should comport themselves in such a manner, as to be recognized as ladies by the *grandes dames* of the aristocracy. In all matters of etiquette the French ladies of the seventeenth century were far in advance of the women of other nations of those times.

It was not pure conceit on the part of Voltaire to write in a letter to an English friend: «de toutes les nations la française est celle qui a le plus connu la société». And it was also true in France that: «la société dépend des femmes».[1] In the social intercourse between the personages who figure in Corneille's dramas, we see distinctly the influence of polite society, and in no point more distinctly than in the mode of address which they employ towards one another. In all languages it is a well known custom that lovers, intimate friends and members of the same family address each other in the second person singular. This is a custom which springs, as it were, from the heart. But the conventions of polite society have more to do with the head than with the heart. Thus it is that in Corneille's early plays, we see the second person singular, the «tu» gradually disappearing in favor of the more formal «vous». Chimène, Camille and Émilie still address their adorers as «thou»; but even as far back as that, the ideas of *bienséance* had forbidden the men to take a like liberty towards the ladies. Curiace and Cinna invariably say «vous»; Rodrigue also, though in one instance he makes bold to address Chimène with «tu».[2] Émilie is the last heroine to address her lover in the second person singular, and even here it is the language of superiority, rather than of affection. With the appearance on the scene of the loving and lovable Pauline, we expect to hear the real language of love, from her lips. But by this time an inexorable *bienséance* had decreed for all time that tragic heroes and heroines, whatever their relation, must meet strictly on terms of «vous».

The same ideas of *bienséance* which forbade the use of

---

[1] Voltaire, Seconde Lettre à M. Falkener. 2. Edition of Zaïre.
[2] Le Cid 3 IV. Compare int his scene 1. 850. «Assurez-vous l'honneur de m'empêcher de vivre» and 1. 853. N'épargnez point mon sang, goûtez, sans résistance.» Notice that the remainder of the speeches of Rodrigue in this scene are in the second person singular.

endearing language between lovers, quite naturally prevented the display of all other marks of affection. Gallant compliments were always in order, but the lover's kiss was tabooed. Fontenelle congratulated his nation that the habit of kissing upon the stage disappeared with the *bourgeois* heroines of Alexandre Hardy. Thus it is that Rodrigue and Chimène, Curiace and Camille, Polyeucte and Pauline hold each other at arms' length or to be more exact, they do not come into contact at all. A Romeo and Juliet would have been impossible on the French stage. And it took nearly two hundred years, before the French public were ready to welcome, with rapture the tender, clinging Doṅa Sol of Victor Hugo's *Hernani*. Today Chiméne and Dona Sol, these two Spanish heroines, born on French soil form in equal measure the delight of the foremost actresses of the Théâtre Français.

It remains in this connection to speak of one more requirement exacted by a strenuous *bienséance*. The stage of the seventeenth century made no attempt to rival the local color of our nineteenth century productions. The Cléopatre of Corneille was not the Cléopatre of Sardou. She did not bid for applause by means of archaeological costuming or spectacular surroundings. She appeared in the full skirt and low cut bodice of the seventeenth century, with the anachronism, also commited by the Cléopatre [1] of Shakespeare of wearing stays. But she pleased the noble ladies of the epoch, as did the young Spanish girl, the Parthian Princess and the queen of Carthage by conforming to their ideas of good taste. As for the heroes of antiquity, they proved to be admirable foils to the heroines. Their manners were perfect. Let one example suffice: Polyeucte, the Christian martyr, before offering up his prayer, first drew off his white gloves and removed the plumed hat which covered his long periwig.[2]

---

[1] Antony and Cleopatra 1 III 71.
[2] For full particulars concerning the stage productions before and after the time of Corneille, see:

5. Their Gallic Wit.

We have called attention to the elegance of the Corneille heroine in her manners, as a result of the etiquette of the times, and also to the choiceness of her language which reflects the influence of the affected Marini and the pompous Gongora. These two elements, encouraged as they were, by the Hôtel Rambouillet, made themselves felt in the heroines of Corneille. But they could not completely conceal the underlying Gallic temperament of the great Corneille. Look through his complete works, and you will see that it is not alone in his comedies, that his native wit shines forth. His tragedies are full of bright touches, telling strokes of wit and sarcasm, and these often appear in persons and in situations where we least expect them. They are precisely those touches of *esprit* which one must have at command today if one hopes to mingle with success in polite French society and what is true today was just as true two hundred years ago. Thus it happens that a captive princess thirsting for revenge often descends to a comedy basis. Comedy lines and comedy situations abound in Corneille. Voltaire writes in speaking of the *Cid*: «On avait cru longtemps en France qu'on ne pouvait supporter le tragique continu sans mélange d'aucune familiarité». The famili-

---

Petit de Julleville. *Histoire du Théâtre en France*. Paris 1880. 3 vol.
Eugène Despois. Le Théâtre Français sous Louis XIV. Paris 1874.
Fournier. *Le Théâtre Français au 16ᵉ et au 17ᵉ siècle*. Paris 1880. 2 vol.
Eugène Rigal. *Esquisse d'une histoire des théâtres de Paris de 1548 à 1635. Hôtel de Bourgogne et Marais*, Paris 1887.
Adolf Ebert. *Entwickelungsgeschichte der französischen Tragödie*. Gotha 1856.
Ferdinand Lotheissen: *Geschichte der französischen Literatur im XVII. Jahrhundert*. vol. II. p. 375. Vienna 1879.

arities in the language of Corneille's characters, however, were never of a low order. His people were too well bred to go below the level of high comedy. Corneille's was the wit of the wellbred Frenchman. In translating the *Agamemnon* of his favorite Seneca, his politeness would never have permitted Clytemnestra to call Electra by such a vulgar name as «babouine», as Rolland Brisset had done in 1589. Nor would he have allowed his Sophonisbe to be denounced by her husband in such comparatively mild terms as «impudente» and «effrontée», as Mairet had done even as late as 1629. And in the year of the Cid, he would never have deigned to deal in such trivialities as did Scudéry in his *Didon*, where the queen of Carthage is summoned from the grotto by Aeneas in the following puerile language :

>Madame, il ne pleut plus; votre majesté sorte

and is informed of the arrival of her sister and her suite by the announcement of the hero :

>Holà! hi! L'on répond, la voix est déjà proche
>Hola! hi! La voicy!

The pleasantries of Corneille's personages turn largely upon the marriage relation, and at critical moments they seem always ready with malicious insinuatious. Sabine, for example, after a plaintive exposition of her pathetic situation, gossips with her confidant about her brother's betrothed :

>Hier *dans sa belle humeur*, elle entretint Valère
>
>Horace 1 I 111.

This bantering tone is then taken up by the confidant, who teases Camille on the same subject :

>Vous déguisez en vain une chose trop claire :
>*Je vous vis encore hier entretenir Valère ;*
>Et l'accueil gracieux qu'il recevoit de vous
>Lui permet de nourrir un espoir assez doux —

Camille.
>Si je l'entretins hier et *lui fis bon visage*,
>N'en imaginez rien qu'à son désavantage:
>>*Horace* 1 II 159—64.

This conversation takes place on the eve of the great struggle between Alba and Rome. We have already called attention to the manner in which Horace, Sabine and Julie discuss their tears and speculate upon the possibilities of Camille's finding another lover to replace the fallen Curiace, and we have also seen how the same arguments are made to do service in the case of Andromède and Suréna.

Let us pass on to another aspect of the marriage relation, as it appears in Corneille. We know that Rodelinde seeks her «*gloire*» in the fidelity with which she cherishes the memory of her presumably deceased husband. The intriguing Eduïge, however, fearing that Rodelinde may be having secret designs on the tyrant Grimoald, determines to forestall the matter without delay, and this she does in the following tone:

>Mais quelquefois, Madame, avec facilité
>On croit des maris morts qui sont pleins de santé;
>Et lorsqu'on se prépare aux seconds hyménées
>*On voit par leur retour des veuves étonnées*
>>*Pertharite* 1 II 145—48.

Excellent comedy lines for the right comedy situation, but unjust as used to degrade the dignity of a noble woman like Rodelinde, merely to show off the wit of Eduïge.

Sophonisbe's devotion to Carthage causes her to abandon her husband Syphax in order to enter into a politico-matrimonial alliance with Massinissa. The arguments by which the heroine is won over, are couched in the elegant language of high comedy. Massinissa says to her:

>En un mot le triomphe est un supplice aux reines;
>La femme du vaincu ne le peut éviter,
>Mais celle du vainqueur n'a rien à redouter.
>*De l'une il est aisé que vous deveniez l'autre;*
>>*Sophonisbe* 2 IV 625—28.

After Sophonisbe has taken the decisive step, the Roman consul consoles the forsaken husband by predicting that she too will probably be served in the same way before long; for, as he reasons:

> Si l'hymen fut trop prompt, le divorce est aisé.
> Sophonisbe envers vous l'ayant mis en usage,
> Le recevra de lui *sans changer de visage,*
>
> *Sophonisbe* 4 II 1232—34.

These lines are more suggestive of the intriguing heroine of high comedy than of a queen, who has come down to posterity as a model of self-sacrifice and devotion to her fatherland.

Plautine in *Othon* is also compromised by being made the subject of undignified dialogue. Othon declares that his love for her is so great that he should die of grief, if she were to be taken from him; whereat the Roman consul reminds him with a slight tinge of maliciousness of the fortitude with which he bore up, when his previous wife, Poppée was taken from him. He says:

> Poppée avoit pour vous du moins autant d'appas;
> Et quand on vous l'ôta, vous n'en mourûtes pas.
>
> *Othon* 1 II 191—92.

Pauline, in despair at the little effect which her tears have on Polyeucte, remarks to her confidant:

> Tu vois, ma Stratonice, en quel siècle nous sommes:
> *Voilà notre pouvoir sur les esprits des hommes;*
>
> *Polyeucte* 1 III 129—30.

Twenty-three years later, Corneille's original heroine Éryxe expresses a similar conviction:

> Ici nous ne savons encore ce que nous sommes:
> *Je tiens tout fort douteux tant qu'il dépend des hommes,*
>
> *Sophonisbe* 2 II 547—48.

Attila on four different occasions pays rapturous tribute to the beautiful eyes of Ildione. But this princess, jealous of the attentions which he is paying to her rival, Honorie, finds herself obliged to remind him:

> J'ai des yeux verront ce qu'il me faudra voir.
> *Attila* 3 II 925.

Honorie too plays an unwilling part in a comedy situation. Resisting the presumptuous advances of Attila, she does not attempt to conceal the scorn which a Roman princess should feel for a barbarian tyrant. Drawing herself up to her full height, she gives utterance to one of those grandiloquent truths, which Corneille was wont to place upon the lips of his heroines:

> Les grands coeurs parlent avec franchise.
> *Attila* 3 IV 1070.

What is her consternation to have this noble sentiment thrown back at her as a joke in the next act! Her words so irritated Attila, that like Sertorius in the case of Viriate five years before, he determined to humble the haughty beauty by imposing upon her a marriage unworthy of her «*gloire*», and prejudicial to her political interests. At her cry of surprise, Attila pays her back in her own words:

> Les grands coeurs parlent avec franchise
> *C'est une vérité que vous m'avez apprise:*
> *Attila* 4 III 1237—38.

Voltaire considers the tragedy of *Attila* so pitiable that, as he says, his readers would never pardon him, if he had wasted precious time in writing a commentary on it. As Voltaire's strong point was his literary style, it would have been interesting to see how he would have criticised the rhyme in which Attila threatens Ildione:

> Souvenez vous enfin que je suis *Attila*,
> Et que c'est dire tout que d'aller *jusque-là*
> *Attila* 3 II 891—92.

The triviality of the rhyme unwittingly brings Attila down to the plane of a king of vaudeville, and Sophonisbe becomes a queen of burlesque, when she allows herself to be wooed by a mélange of figurative and literal language. After her first husband has been made prisoner, Massinisse wins her over by reminding her:

> Et sa captivité qui rompt cet hyménée
> Laisse votre main libre et *la sienne enchaînée*.
> *Sophonisbe* 2 IV 643—44.

Plautine becomes a *bourgeois* heroine of comedy, when after nobly sacrificing her own love for Othon, and begging him for the good of the State to sue for the hand of Camille, she asks coyly of her confidant:

> Dis-moi, donc lorsqu'Othon s'est offert à Camille,
> A-t-il paru contraint? *a-t-elle été facile?*
> *Othon* 2 I 373—74.

We do not take serious offence at Chimène for introducing a pun into one of her reflections concerning the good of the State:

> Mourir pour le pays n'est pas un triste sort;
> C'est s'immortaliser par une belle *mort*,
> *Le Cid* 4 V 1367—68.

nor with the Infante, in the midst of the despair by which she is racked, for playing upon words:

> Ma plus douce *espérance* est de perdre *l'espoir*
> *Le Cid* 1 II 135.

a famous line condemned by Scudéry, but applauded by the Académie Française.

But when the queen of Lemnos archly remarks to the enchantress Medea:

> Je n'ai que des *attraits*, et vous avez des *charmes*.
> *La Toison d'Or* 3 IV 1285.

we forget that *The Golden Fleece* is a tragedy of the great Corneille. His tragic heroines seem more like two operetta queens of Offenbach.

8

Corneille's Gallic vivacity of temperament is well shown in his treatment of Chimène's fainting scene an episode borrowed from the *Cid* of Castro. In the French drama, the young girl is informed of the death of her lover. She turns pale and gasps:

> Quoi! Rodrigue est donc mort?
> D. Fernand.
> Non, non, il voit le jour
> Et te conserve encore un immuable amour:
> Calme cette douleur qui pour lui s'intéresse.

To which Chimène retorts:

> Sire, on pâme de joie ainsi que de tristesse:
> *Le Cid* 4 V 1347—50.

The ready reply of the heroine recovering from a swoon is quite in contrast to that of the dignified Jimena of the Spanish Cid. Castro's heroine, in the ponderous measures of the Spanish verse, says, in the body of a long speech:

> Tante atribula un placer
> Como congoja un pesar
> Castro. *Las Mocedades del Cid.* Jornada III escena 1.

Corneille's Chimène, more vivacious, expresses the same idea, as we have seen, in a single line, and thus brings her retort into rhyme with the preceding speech of the king.

We have already called attention to the scene of pithy dialogue between Sophonisbe and Éryxe, where the latter prides herself on having «a little common sense». This touch of sarcasm would seem to have its origin in Corneille's own mood at the time of writing. It will be remembered that in 1660, the poet issued an edition of his works, in which the celebrated *Examens* appeared for the first time. In 1663, the year of *Sophonisbe*, a second edition appeared, in which Corneille says, as if to his in creasing number of detractors, that his only guide in writing his first play was «un peu de sens commun». The mood of Corneille in this every day expression would therefore, seem to have passed over into his ideal queen of Getulia. But this is constantly recurring in literature. Characters are often made to say whatever is uppermost in the mind of the author. Oftentimes too, a remote personage like a queen of Getulia can be made to express sentiments that an author would hardly dare to be responsible for in his quality as an ordinary citizen. During the Fronde, as is well known, the heroines of Corneille produced their strongest impression on women like the Duchesse de Longueville, the Duchesse de Chevreuse, the Princesse Palatine and Mademoiselle Montpensier, who through the medium of Corneille's own personality, saw themselves mirrored to the life. The heroines of Corneille were thoroughly in touch with the heroines of the Fronde.

Another instance of Corneille's own humor is the sarcastic tone in which he trifles with the chief catchword of his heroines. On being congratulated by Boileau on the glory of his long career, he is said to have replied drily, «Je suis saoul de *gloire* et affamé d'argent».

With these unmistakable evidences of a comedy element in the situations and personages of Corneille, it is difficult to account for an opinion recently expressed, that the poet, on reaching the age of thirty, «change de voie. il semble avoir oublié l'art comique». [1] It is true that with the exception of *Le Menteur*, Corneille did not produce any more comedies, but that did not prevent his comedy vein from asserting itself, as we have shown, in the serious dramas of his later days. It would be quite as reasonable to deny the presence of the tragic or heroic element in the comedies of Corneille. To quote but a single example in the comedy *L'Illusion*, Matamoras boasts of himself:

> *Le seul bruit de mon nom renverse les murailles,*
> *Défait les escadrons, gagne les batailles.*

---

[1] M. le Comte de Moüy. Les Comédies de Corneille. La Nouvelle Revue. 1 Sept. 1896.

> Mon courage invaincu contre les empereurs
> N'arme que la moitié de ses moindres fureurs;
>
> *L'Illusion* 2 II 233—36.

And Boileau in 1672, did not hesitate to appropriate these ideas, and incorporate them almost literally into his eulogy of Louis de Bourbon, prince de Condé, one of the greatest heroes of his times:

> *Condé dont le seul nom fait tomber les murailles*
> *Force les escadrons, et gagne les batailles.*
>
> Boileau *Epître* IV au Roi 133—84.

No, the comedy element in Corneille's tragedies is to be traced directly back to the native wit of the poet himself. He was not always sublime and sombre. In those bright flashes of wit, which take us often by surprise, we recognize not «le grand Corneille», but Corneille the national Frenchman.

In the course of the present essay, we have had occasion to refer often to the commentaries of Voltaire on Corneille. In the present connection, these commentaries have a peculiar interest in that they show us the nobler side of Voltaire's nature, and at the same time his innate «*méchanceté*», to use a word, the peculiar flavor of which it is hard to translate. As the reader knows, the proceeds of Voltaire's edition of Corneille with commentaries were to go to Mlle. Marie Corneille, grand-niece of the poet. Voltaire's motives were generous, but he, nevertheless, allowed no opportunity of holding Corneille up to ridicule to pass unimproved. He wilfully misconstrued the meaning of many lines, especially where he saw the chance of suggesting a *double entendre*. For instance, when the sentimental queen Laodice says to Nicomède:

> Après tant de hauts faits, il m'est bien doux, Seigneur,
> De voir encor mes yeux régner sur votre coeur;
>
> *Nicomède* 1 I 1—2.

Voltaire comments maliciously «On ne voit point ses yeux».

In like manner Émilie[1] and Pauline[2] are held up to ridicule by the *méchant* comments of Voltaire.

The question as to how far the comic element should be allowed to enter into a tragedy needs not be discussed here. We would only call the attention of the reader to the fact that the comic of Corneille is not the grotesque comic which we find in the tragedies of Victor Hugo who imitates the familiar comic of Shakspeare. It is always the refined comic, which at its best would not have been unworthy of Molière. It was the comic of the seventeenth century in France.

The naiveté of the French wit is one of its greatest charms. The art of saying little but of suggesting much has been carried to perfection by the French. Back in the middle ages their ready wit was as keen as it is today. The unknown poet who wrote the *Mystère d'Adam*, adapted his biblical story to the temperament of his listeners, by allowing Eve to address Adam in a saucy, vivacious tone. At the critical moment when he is hesitating as to whether he had better taste the forbidden fruit, he asks ingenuously «Est-il tant bon?» and Eve replies, in a couplet:

              Tu le savras
Nel poez saver, sin gusteras.

And with this genuine touch of nature in a work otherwise solemn and serious, the mediaeval poet reached the heart and the understanding of his public. He too would have agreed with Victor Hugo that nature and art are one and inseparable.[3]

---

[1] Remarques sur Cinna 1 III.
[2] Remarques sur Polyeucte 1 III.
[3] Victor Hugo. Préface de Cromwell.

6. Their personal charms and attributes.

The final requisite of the Corneille heroine is her beauty. In the estimation of the poet it was highly desirable that his heroines should be as beautiful as the ladies who applauded them. Feminine beauty, to be sure, has always been a favorite theme with the poets of all nations. But in the seventeenth century Corneille found himself constrained by his ideas of good taste and *bienséance*, and also by his reverence for the canons of of Malherbe, to make his heroines beautiful, according to rule. In the Middle Ages, it had been the custom of the poets to rhapsodize in detail over the many charms of their adored ones.[1] Back in the twelfth century, Nicolette is described as follows:

>Vo vair oeil et vos gens cors
>Vos biax ris et dox mos
>Ont men cuer navré a mort
>
>23. 13—15.

In another place:

>Nicolete est avene toi
>M'amiete o le bont poil
>
>25. 3—4.

And again:

>Nicolete o le vis cler
>
>13. 1.

and we are informed that «des cheveux blonds et un teint transparent constituent au moyen âge l'idéal de beauté, surtout pour les hommes du Nord».[2] But of this wealth of detail, in which Nicolette is described, Corneille seems to have appropriated for his heroines only the beautiful eyes; which invest his political princesses with a pastoral charm, which

---

[1] See Aucassin et Nicolete. Suchier Edition Paderborn 1889.
[2] L. Constans. Supplement à la Chrestomathie de l'Ancien Français p. 51. Paris 1885.

must have made them very pleasing to the aristocratic society of the seventeenth century, when the pastoral novel of the school of d'Urfé was at the zenith of its popularity. The «beaux yeux» of Corneille's heroines are sometimes made the object of a compliment on the part of a lover, or quite as often it is the heroine herself, who with her wonted self-possession tells us of the power of her eyes and the great deeds which they accomplish.

Curiously enough we find in Corneille's *Cid* no mention of the heroine's beautiful eyes, notwithstanding the fact that in the Spanish original, Rodrigo says of his Jimena:

>De sus *ojos soberanos*
>Siento en el alma el disgusto
>>Castro. *Las Moredades del Cid* Jornada II escena 2.

But Corneille more than made good this omission in his following works, as we shall see.

The beautiful eyes of Camille, for example, almost deter Curiace from the contest between Alba and Rome. As he listens to the pleadings of his betrothed, he muses:

>Que les pleurs d'une amante ont de puissants discours,
>Et qu'*un bel oeil* est fort avec un tel secours!
>>*Horace* 2 V 576—77.

Polyeucte is similary affected in presence of Pauline. Almost shaken in his determination to become a Christian, he says to his mentor:

>Et mon coeur, attendri sans être intimidé
>N'ose déplaire aux yeux dont il est possédé.
>. . . . .
>Sur mes pareils, Néarque, *un bel oeil* est bien fort:
>>*Polyeucte* 1 I 19—87.

It is the same reflection which restrains Maxime, a rival suitor for the hand of Émilie, from betraying Cinna to Augustus:

>Ce n'est pas le moyen de *plaire à ses beaux yeux*
>Que de priver du jour ce qu'elle aime le mieux.
>>*Cinna* 3 I 771—72.

Cléopatre describes the power of her eyes over the great Caesar:

> Son bras ne dompte point de peuples ni de lieux
> Dont *il ne rend hommage au pouvoir de mes yeux;*
>
> *Pompée* 2 I 395—96.

and nineteen years later, the eyes of Médée exert the same influence over Jason. Proudly she says:

> De tout ce qu'il a fait de grand, de glorieux,
> *Il rend un plein hommage au pouvoir de mes yeux.*
>
> *La Toison d'Or* 1 I 307—8.

Caesar himself acknowledges to Cléopatre the wonderful power of her beautiful eyes:

> Et *vos beaux yeux* enfin m'ayant fait soupirer,
> . . . .
> M'ont rendu le premier et de Rome et du monde.
>
> *Pompée* 4 III 1276—78.

Absyrte addresses Hypsipyle in similar gallant language:

> Madame, si j'osois, dans le trouble où vous êtes.
> Montrer à *vos beaux yeux* des peines plus secrètes,
>
> *La Toison d'Or* 2 V 964—65.

The beautiful eyes of Pulchérie drive Héraclius to take the life of the tyrant Phocas:

> Et *ces yeux tout divins,* par un soudain pouvoir,
> Achevèrent sur moi l'effet de ce devoir.
>
> *Héraclius* 2 II 527—28.

The three idyllic nymphs of Andromède have beautiful eyes in real pastoral style, but they have tried their power on Persée to no purpose. Andromède reproaches them:

> Ah! c'est de quoi rougir toutes avec justice;
> Et la honte à vos fronts doit bien cette couleur.
> Si *tant de beaux yeux* ont pu manquer son coeur.
>
> *Andromède* 2 I 487-89.

Andromède's beautiful eyes are thus prettily sung by Liriope:

> Enfin si *ses beaux yeux* passent pour un miracle,
> C'est un miracle aussi que son amour.
>
> *Andromède* 2 II 562—63.

Rodelinde, after listening to several compliments, and having declared to the tyrant, who wishes to marry her:

> Jamais d'un *seul coup d'oeil* je t'ai fait espérer ;
> *Pertharite* 1 III 238.

at last declares scornfully :

> On publieroit de toi que *les yeux d'une femme*
> Plus que ta propre gloire auroient touché ton âme
> *Pertharite* 2 V 671—72.

The fidelity of Rodelinde, merited indeed that Pertharite on his return should beg the privilege of dying before her eyes. He says to her:

> Le ciel, qui vous destine à régner en ces lieux,
> M'accorde au moins le bien de *mourir à vos yeux.*
> *Pertharite* 4 V 1425—26.

This had previously been the ambition of Maxime and Sevère, to die respectively before the eyes of Émilie and Pauline, Corneille was so much impressed with this idea that on his return to the theatre after an absence of nearly ten years, he made it a feature of the gallant love of Thésée for the newly invented princess Dircé, introduced for the first time by Corneille into the Oedipus tragedy. Thesée says to her:

> Ici je puis mourir, mais *mourir à vos yeux* ;
> *Oedipe* 1 I 40.

Sophonisbe reflects on what the power of her eyes has accomplished. With her rival Éryxe in mind she says:

> *Mes yeux* d'une autre reine *ont détruit le pouvoir !*
> *Sophonisbe* 2 V 728—29.

By a process of analogy, it would seem as if Corneille had allowed this idea to pass over into his next drama, for Plautine with one glance causes Othon to forget all previous flames. He tells her:

> Vous seule *d'un coup' d'oeil* emportâtes la gloire
> D'en faire évanouir la plus douce mémoire,
> *Othon* 2 II 485—86.

Attila, hesitating in his choice between Honorie and Ildione, reflects:

> *Que chacun de leurs yeux* aime à se faire esclave ;
> Moi, je ne veux les voir qu'en tyrans que je brave:
> *Attila* 1 II 125—28.

Attila, nevertheless, succumbs to the inevitable. The beauty of Ildione gets the mastery of him, and he cries:

> Cruel poison de l'âme, et *doux charmes des yeux*,
> . . . .
> *Ses yeux*, mes souverains, à qui tout est soumis,
> *ibid.* 3 I 764—79.
> Défendez *à vos yeux* cet éclat invincible.
> *ibid.* 3 II 841.

To appease Ildione for the love which political interests prevent him from bestowing on her. Attila offers to make her queen of a part of Gaule, as a final tribute to her beautiful eyes. He makes the following proposition:

> Si la Gaule vous plaît, vous la partagerez :
> J'en offre la conquête *à vos yeux adorés* ;
> *ibid.* 3 II 875—76.

Ildione, however, is not to be bought over by a compromise. In her next monologue, after the manner of Chimène, she apostrophizes the eyes, which have held such sway over Attila, but which begin to show signs of losing their power:

> Trêve, *mes tristes yeux*, trêve aujourd'hui de larmes !
> Armez contre un tyran *vos plus dangéreux charmes :*
> *Attila* 4 VII 1437—38.

In contrast to the idyllic sentimental mood of Corneille in regard to the beautiful eyes of his heroine, is the Gallic vivacity with which he invests Viriate's reply to Sertorius in their first political interview:

> Et je veux bien, Seigneur, qu'on sache désormais
> Que *j'ai d'assez bons yeux pour voir ce que je fais*
> *Sertorius* 2 II 523—24.

It is the same ironical touch, which Honorie five years later, puts into her reply to Attila:

J'ai des yeux qui verront ce qu'il me faudra voir.
Attila 3 II 925.

another mingling of the pastoral and the comic element in the tragedy of Corneille.

The foregoing examples are not the only ones,[1] to be found in Corneille, but the number is sufficient to show the poet's fondness for beautiful eyes, and to establish them as quite the most important charm of his tragic heroines; and indeed not only of Corneille's heroines, but of the heroines in general of the French classic drama after Corneille. The beautiful eyes of the revengeful Hermione in Racine's *Andromaque*

---

[1] Compare further:
a) Chalciope, assuring Médée of Jason's devotion to her. *La Toison d'Or* 1 I 313—14.
    Oui, je l'ai vu moi-même,
    Que *pour plaire à vos yeux* il prend un soin extrême;
b) Seleucus, speaking with the confidant of Rodogune, *Rodogune* 1 II 97—100.
    Et vous, en ma faveur, voyez ce cher objet,
    Et tâchez *d'abaisser ses yeux* sur un sujet
    Qui peut-être aujourd'hui porteroit la couronne
    S'il n'attachoit les siens à sa seule personne,
c) Théodore, banishing her lover from her sight, *Théodore* 2 II 405.
    Je crains d'en recevoir *quelque coup d'oeil fatal*,
d) Laodice greeting Nicomède in *Nicomède* 1 I 1—2.
    Après tants de hauts faits, il m'est bien doux, Seigneur,
    De voir encore mes yeux régner sur votre coeur;
e) the confidant of Grimoald, pleading the cause of his sovereign before Rodelinde in *Pertharite* 1 I 73—74.
    Excusez un amour que *vos yeux ont éteint*:
    Son coeur pour Eduïge en étoit lors atteint;
f) Eduïge complimented by Grimoald in *Pertharite* 5 II 1621—22.
    Et dans ce coeur à vous *par vos yeux combattu*
    Tout mon amour s'oppose à toute ma vertu.
g) the précieuse language of Attila to Ildione in *Attila* 3 II 823—24.
    Mes plus heureux succès ne font qu'enfoncer mieux
    L'inévitable trait dont me percent vos yeux.
h) the magnanimous compliment of Palmis to her rival Eurydice in *Suréna* 1 II 214—15.
    Si l'ingrat me trahit, *vos yeux le justifient*,
    Vos yeux qui sur moi-même ont un tel ascendant . . .

drive Orestet o attempt the life of Pyrrhus; and even the Queen Elizabeth of Thomas Corneille's *Comte d'Essex* in a fit of despair at being forsaken by the hero of the piece, cries out:

> Il a trop de ma bouche, *il a trop de mes yeux.*
> Thomas Corneille. *Le Comte d'Essex* 2 I.

This piece was produced in 1678, before the death of the elder Corneille, and this trait of the heroine cannot fail to have met with his entire approval. The student of English history, however, cannot quite forget that at the time when the play is supposed to have taken place, Elizabeth was according to the dates of history fifty eight years old, and her beautiful eyes strike him as a little anachronistic. But Pierre and Thomas Corneille were not troubled by any such quibbles. Indeed the Pulchérie of 1672 but a few years before had been wooed by a lover who went into ecstasy over: «ce charme de vos yeux». And Corneille tells us naively in his preface *Au Lecteur*: «Elle passoit alors cinquante ans, et mourut deux ans après».

There is no doubt that Corneille was as susceptible to the charm of beautiful eyes as the heroes of his tragedies. Indeed, but for Mlle. Milet of Rouen, whose beautiful eyes inspired him to write his first play, the comedy of *Mélite*, Corneille might never have chosen the career of dramatist. He tells us:

> Mon bonheur commença, quand mon âme fut prise
> Je gagnai de la gloire en perdant ma franchise
> *Charmé de deux beaux yeux*, mon vers charma la cour
> Et ce que j'ai de nom, je le dois à l'amour
> *Excuse à Ariste* 61—64.

This was in 1629. Thirty years later in 1659, the beautiful eyes of Mlle. du Parc of Molière's troupe brought Corneille back to the theatre, after seven years of retirement, but this time it was a tragedy which they produced. In the vainglorious style not only permissible but customary among the the writers of the seventeenth century, Corneille sums up the great services, which he has done for the stage, and reminds

Mlle. du Parc, the Marquise as she was called, that his great talents still:

> pourront sauver la gloire
> *Des yeux qui me semblent doux*
>
> Stances à une Marquise.

This gallantry, however, must not be taken too seriously. Voltaire after the performance of his tragedy *Zaïre* addressed a similar effusion to the young actress, who appeared in the title rôle, in which he paid tribute no less than three times to her eyes:

> Ce sont *tes yeux*, ces yeux si pleins de charmes
> . . . .
> Le dieu d'amour . . . .
> Est par *tes yeux* bien plus sûr de régner
> . . . .
> Que tu reçois avec un sourire tendre
> Qui voit son sort écrit *dans tes beaux yeux*.
>
> Voltaire. *Epître à Mlle Gaussin.*

There is no doubt that the use and abuse of «beaux yeux» were recognized even in the seventeenth century. That they must have become a part of the poetical jargon of every rhymester is evidenced by the fact that Molière, with his keen sense of the ridiculous, allowed his *Bourgeois Gentilhomme* to be edified by the following effusion, in the conventional sentimental language of the times:

> Je languis nuit et jour, et mon mal est extrême
> Depuis qu'à vos rigueurs *vos beaux yeux* m'ont soumis.
> Si vous traitez ainsi, belle Iris, qui vous aime
> Hélas! que pourriez-vous faire à vos ennemis!
>
> *Le Bourgeois Gentilhomme.* 1 II.

We can almost hear Attila sighing for the beautiful Ildione, the last of Corneille's heroines to appear on the scene previous to the *Bourgeois Gentilhomme*.

But there is still another explanation of the constant recurrence of beautiful eyes in the French tragedy. If we care to examine the sentimental poetry of the Middle Ages, we shall find that they are a favorite theme of the old troubadours. To quote but a single example, Bernart de Ventadorn[1] in the year 1154 complains of the coldness of Eleonore of Poitou:

> So lo be quem prezenta
> Sos bels olhs el francs vis

Chrestien de Troies makes it clearer to us how the Thésée of Corneille's *Oedipe* was «wounded» by the eyes of Dircé. Thésée confesses his love for the princess as follows:

> Thésée
> En un mot, c'est leur soeur, la princesse Dircé,
> Dont les yeux . . .
> Oedipe.
> Quoi? ses yeux, Prince, vous ont blessé?
> *Oedipe* 1 II 155—56.

In a long passage in the *Cligès* of Chrestien,[2] Alexandre soliloquizes with himself as to the cause and nature of his passion for Soredamors. He tells us that he is severely wounded. Then he asks himself why the wound is not visible, and explains the reason in the following poetic manner: Cupid takes his bow and arrow and shoots his victim in the eye, whence the dart descends to the heart and leaves an aching wound. Why is the eye not wounded? Because it is only a mirror which lights the way to the heart. The musings of Alexandre over the wanton wiles of the little God of Love form one of the gems of mediaeval literature. The idea was an old one. Chrestien develops it with the impetuousness which characterizes a literature in its infancy. Corneille writing under quite different circumstances treats the idea with full regard for the exigencies required by the bienséance of his century. In two methodically rhymed Alexandrine verses, the manner of Dircé's fascinations for Thésée are described. Her beautiful eyes were a part of her birthright as a heroine of Corneille.

The beautiful eyes of the Corneille heroine make the

---

[1] See Bartsch's Chrestomathie Provençale p. 50.
[2] Cligès 692—724. Förster edition.

strongest impression on us because they are the only concrete charms with which Corneille endows her. He had at command, however, a number of other stereotyped attributes of a gallant nature, which he applied systematically to his heroines. In the *Cid* and *Horace* these epithets are conspicuous by their absence, but in *Cinna* they begin and with *Pompée* the list is practically complete. The poet feels that he has invented or at least adopted a sufficient number of epithets, with which to equip his heroines.

Let us begin with Émilie. Cinna, summing up the situation at Rome, says to her;

> Voilà, *belle Émilie*, à quel point nous en sommes.
> *Cinna* 1 III 249.

Later in the play, Maxime addresses her in the same terms:
> Vivez, *belle Émilie*,
> *ibid.* 4 V 1389.

Cinna reflecting on the goodness of Augustus, prays that Emilie may be brought to relent:
> Plût aux Dieux . . . .
> Que sa bonté touchât *la beauté* qui me charme,
> *ibid.* 3 II 799—801.

Still hesitating to undertake the awful deed which Emilie demands of him, he says to her:
> Et si je ne vous aime avec toute l'ardeur
> Que peut *un digne objet* attendre d'un grand coeur!
> . . . .
> Mais l'empire inhumain qu'exercent *vos beautés*
> *ibid.* 3 IV 927—1055.

Augustus in the same terms as Cinna describes his adopted daughter:
> . . . . Émilie,
> Le *digne objet* des voeux de toute l'Italie,
> *ibid.* 5 I 1469—70.

And even after discovering the conspiracy of which she formed the head, he does not lose his aplomb, but pays her a direct compliment. After making peace with Cinna in those well known words «Soyons amis, Cinna», which are said to have moved the great Condé and Louis XIV to tears, Augustus continues:

> Avec *cette beauté* que je t'avois donnée,
> Reçois le consulat pour la prochaine année.
>
> *ibid.* 5 III 1709—10.

Pauline offers a few new examples of Corneille's favorite epithets. Her lover, Sévère on beholding her, exclaims:

> Ah! quelle comble de joie
> *Cette chère beauté* consent que je la voie!
>
> *Polyeucte* 2 I 373—74.

In the cource of their interview, he addresses her:

> O *trop aimable objet*, qui m'avez trop charmé,
>
> *ibid.* 2 II 495.

and he takes leave of her with the words:

> Adieu, *trop vertueux objet*, et trop charmant.
>
> *ibid.* 2 II 571

If now to the foregoing, we add a gallant couplet which first appears in *Pompée* we shall have enumerated the most important of Corneille's favorite epithets. Caesar and Marc Antony compare notes on Cleopatra:

> César
> Antoine, avez-vous vu cette reine *adorable*?
> Antoine
> Oui, seigneur, je l'ai vue: elle est *incomparable*;
>
> *Pompée* 3 III 945—46.

A glance through the works of Corneille will show that he had an undisguised preference for the word «belle». His heroines were beautiful. It was the easiest way to say so frankly. Compare the following:

> Cléopatre vous hait; elle est fière, *elle est belle*;
>
> *Pompée* 1 IV 345.
> Hypsipyle vous aime, elle est reine, *elle est belle*;
>
> *La Toison d'Or* 3 I 1036.
> Justine a du mérite, elle est jeune, *elle est belle:*
>
> *Pulchérie* 5 VI 1697.

La princesse est mandée, elle vient, *elle est belle;*
Suréna 1 I 117.

Again the reader feels that it was the rhyme, which compelled Corneille to make his heroines beautiful and it is true that the word «belle» does furnish the necessary rhyme for words like «elle», «infidèle» and other words of similar ending.[1] But there are also very many instances in which the word does not stand in rhyme. Compare the following:[2]

---

[1] Compare further:
a) *Attila* 4 IV 1289.
 La princesse Ildione est orgueilleuse et *belle;*
b) *Andromède* 1 I 131
 Andromède jamais ne me parat si *belle;*
c) *Andromède* 2 II 546
 Phinée est plus aimé qu' Andromède n'est *belle,*
d) Hypsipyle in *La Toison d'Or* 4 IV 1672—73
 Abandonnant pour vous une reine si *belle,*
 J'ai poussé par pitié quelques soupirs vers elle:
e) Plautine in *Othon* 2 IV 597
 Après tout, je me trompe, ou près de cette *belle.*
f) Mandane in *Agésilas* 1 IV 366
   Cotys
 Seigneur, l'aimeroit-il?
   Spitridete.
Il la trouve assez *belle.*
g) Bérénice in *Tite et Bérénice* 4 III 1275—76
 Cependant si la Reine, aussi fière que *belle,*
 Sait comme il faut répondre aux voeux d'un infidèle,
h) *Tite et Bérénice* 5 I 1428
 Vous ne me dites plus que Domitie est *belle,*
i) *Agésilas* 2 IV 601
 Ce n'est point qu' Elpinice aux miens n'ait paru *belle;*
j) *Pulchérie* 1 I 145
 Je vois entrer Irène; Aspar la trouve *belle:*
k) Pulchérie in *Pulchérie* 2 I 465
 Je tremblois qu' à leurs yeux elle ne fût trop *belle;*

[2] Compare further:
a) Elpinice and Aglatide in *Agésilas* 1 IV 323.
 Elles aiment ailleurs, *ces belles dédaigneuses;*
b) Bérénice in *Tite et Bérénice* 1 I 116.
 Et *cette belle reine* eut sur lui tant de force,
ibid. 2 I 363.

> Un reste de tendresse
> M'échappe encore au nom *d'une belle princesse;*
> Hypsipyle in *La Toison d'Or* 2 I 684—85.
>
> Puis-je voir sans rougir qu'à *la belle Ildione*
> Vous demandiez congé de m'offrir votre trône,
> *Attila* 4 III 1173—74.
>
> *Car enfin elle est belle*, et digne de ma foi;
> Bérénice in *Tite et Bérénice* 2 I 385.
>
> *Car enfin elle est belle*, elle peut tout séduire
> Ildione in *Attila* 4 IV 1289.

As we have found it interesting to look for analogies in the mediaeval poetry, let us see how the unknown poet of the Chanson de Roland describes the bride of the hero. This one female character plays no important part in the poem. She merely comes to weep over the death of Roland. What interests us here, however, is the language in which she is described: «Alde une bele dame. l. 3708 and the conventional epic formula Alde la bele. l. 3723:[1]

Another proof that Corneille was impressed with the importance of making his heroines beautiful is shown by the fondness with which he also employs the word «beauté». His heroines are beauties:

> Pour *la même beauté* nous faisons mêmes voeux.
> Rodogune in *Rodogune* 1 III 178.
>
> . . . *cette beauté*, qui me tient sous sa loi
> Théodore in *Théodore* 4 V 1473.
>
> Je plaindrois un amant qui suffrait mes peines,
> Et tel pour *deux beautés* que je suis pour deux reines,
> Se verroit déchiré par un égal amour,
> Elvire and Isabelle in *Don Sanche* 2 IV 701—3.
>
> Chez vous est *la beauté* qui fait tous mes souhaits.
> Dircé in *Oedipe* 1 II 152.
>
> Car mon coeur fut son bien à *cette belle reine*
> Et pourroit l'être encor, malgré Rome et sa haine.
> *ibid.* 4 IV 1323—24.
>
> Au moindre empressement pour *cette belle reine*,
> Il vous fera justice et reprendra sa chaîne.

[1] *La Chanson de Roland.* Edition Gautier. Tours 1872.

The supreme selfconsciousness of Domitie allows her to speak of herself as a beauty. She addresses her lover as:

> L'amant digne du coeur de *la beauté* qu'il aime[1]
> *Tite et Bérénice* 4 III 1179.

The five maidens, who were exposed to the sea-monster, before the decree fell on Andromède, are thus described in pastoral language by Cassiope:

> Déja nous avons vu *cinq beautés* devoréés,
> Mais des *beautés*, hélas! dignes d'être adorées,
> *Andromède* 1 I 192—93.

As a final example to prove conclusively Corneille's own enthusiasm for the word, listen to the rhapsody over Ildione, which he puts into the mouth of Attila:

> Je sens combattu encor dans ce coeur qui soupire
> Les droits de la *beauté* contre ceux de l'empire.
> . . . .
> O *beauté*, qui te fais adorer en tous lieux,
> Cruel poison de l'âme, et doux charme des yeux,
> . . . .
> Va la trouver pour moi, *cette beauté charmante*
> *Attila* 3 I 757—69.

We have seen that in the judgment of Caesar and Marc Antony, Cléopatra was declared to be adorable and incomparable. Andromède is a direct successor to the Egyptian queen in this respect:

> Le ciel lui-même en la voyant, charmé
> La juge *incomparable;*

---

[1] Compare further:
a) Rodogune in *Rodogune* 1 II 92.
   . . . pour *cette beauté* je lui cède l'empire;
b) Plautine in *Othon* 1 I 98—99.
   Mon coeur, tout à Plautine, est fermé à Camille.
   La beauté de l'objet, la honte de changer,
c) Pulchérie in *Pulchérie* 2 I 455—56.
   Moi, qui me figurois que ma caducité
   Près de *la beauté* même étoit en sûreté?
d) Hypsipyle in *La Toison d'Or* 3 III 1188.
   Hélas! je ne craignois que *tes beautés de Grèce;*

> Mais quoiqu'il l'ait faite *adorable*,
> Phinée est encor plus aimé.
>
> *Andromède* 2 II 566—69.

Camille is thu described by her rival Plautine:

> Pour vous avec ce trône elle étoit *adorable*,
> Pour vous elle y renonce, et n'a plus rien d'aimable.
>
> *Othon* 4 I 1165.

Thésée sings the charms of the three princesses, mentioned in *Oedipe*:

> Antigone est parfaite, Ismène est *adorable*;
> Dircé, si vous voulez, n'a rien de *comparable*:
> Elles sont l'une et l'autre un chef d'oeuvre des cieux;
>
> *Oedipe* 1 II 161—63.

In the gossip scene with which the daughters of Lysander open the tragedy of *Agésilas*, Elpinice says to Aglatide:

> Et je craindrois fort que Mandane,
> Cette *incomparable* Persane,
> N'eût pour lui des attraits plus forts que vos appas.
>
> *Agésilas* 1 I 153—55.

Andromède is addressed:

> Une seconde fois, *adorable* princesse,
>
> *Andromède* 5 II 1480.

As a final example Attila beseeches Ildione:

> Cessez d'être *adorable*, ...
>
> *Attila* 3 II 839.

We therefore see that Corneille's heroines in rhyme and out of rhyme, were *adorable, aimable, incomparable*.[1]

---

[1] Compare further:
a) Honorie in *Attila* 5 I 1461—62.
    C'est par là que vos yeux la trouvent *adorable*,
    Et que vous faites naître un amour véritable,
b) Elpinice in *Agésilas* 3 III 1172
    Seigneur, la personne est *aimable*:
c) Pulchérie in *Pulchérie* 2 I 469—70
    Quel supplice d'aimer un objet *adorable*
    Et de tant de rivaux se voir le moins aimable!
d) Eurydice in *Suréna* 3 II 854.
    Le prince aime Eurydice autant qu'elle est *aimable*;

Still another term which Corneille applied to his heroines was *objet* with some qualifying adjective, such as *cher, digne, rare, illustre, charmant*. The following examples will serve to illustrate this method:

> Mais lorsqu'*un digne objet* [1] a pu nous enflammer,
> Rodogune in *Rodogune* 1 III 153.
> *Le rare et cher object* qui fait seul mon destin.
> Théodore in *Théodore* 4 I 1129.
> . . . Cet *illustre objet* qui lui blesse les yeux?
> Viriate in *Sertorius* 4 IV 1536.
> Ne vous offensez pas, *objet rare et charmant*, [2]
> Théodore in *Théodore* 2 IV 465.

In *Pompée* we are told of Cleopatra, in her efforts to captivate Caesar:

> . . . . elle s'en vante, elle est son *cher objet*,
> *Pompée* 2 IV 655.

Corneille would seem to have been specially pleased with this method of designating his heroine, for following Cleopatra Rodogune, [3] Théodore, [4] Andromède, [5] Rodelinde, [6] Dircé, [7] So-

---

[1] Compare:
a) Théodore in *Théodore* 2 VI 667.
> . . . ce *digne objet* de votre juste haine
b) Viriate in *Sertorius* 4 II 1261—62.
> Bien qu'un si *digne objet* le rendît excusable,
> J'ai cru honteux d'aimer quand on n'est plus aimable:

[2] Compare:
Rodogune in *Rodogune* 1 III 139—40.
> J'esperois que l'éclat dont le trône se pare
> Toucheroit vos désirs plus qu'un *objet si rare;*

[3] *Rodogune* 1 II 97.
> Et vous, en ma faveur voyez *ce cher objet*,

[4] *Théodore* 4 V 1459—60.
> Hélas! et le moyen d'être sans jalousie,
> Lorsque *ce cher objet* te doit plus que la vie?

[5] *Andromède* 5 I 1441—44.
> Mais de *ce cher objet* s'en voyant plus haï,
> Plus il s'en est flatté plus il s'en croit trahi.

[6] *Pertharite* 5 V 1829.
> Avec *ce cher objet* tout destin m'est doux.

[7] *Oedipe* 1 II 144.

phonisbe,[1] Plautine[2] and Ildione[3] are all described as a «*cher objet*». This is another proof that Corneille was a firm believer in tried methods.

The epithets, which we have enumerated above, are the ones which are indelibly stamped upon the heroines of Corneille. They were the poet's favorite attributes. Every reader knows them. At the same time, it would be doing Corneille an injustice to assert that they are positively the only ones which he made use of, though such an assertion would not be far from the truth. Such expressions as *rare ouvrage, digne image, digne conquête* and *merveille* are also to be met with, expressions *précieuse* and therefore pleasing in the seventeenth century. But in general we must admit that Corneille, though gallant towards his heroines, was nevertheless conservative in his poetical description of their charms.

We have spoken of Corneille's fondness for a pathetic element in his heroines. With the adjective «*triste*» he strove to attain a pathetic end. The bereaved wife of Pompey in *La mort de Pompée* (2 II 537) figures as *la triste Cornélie*. The second wife of Pompey in *Sertorius* (5 II 1636) is mentioned as *la triste Émilie*, and finally the sentimental daughter of Marcelle in *Théodore* (3 V 1063) who likewise is merely mentioned without appearing on the stage, is described as *la triste Flavie*.

The heroines of Corneille have all been designated by Sainte Beuve as *adorables furies*, and this name, from the im-

---

[1] *Sophonisbe* 4 II 1223—24.
　　L'air qu'un si *cher objet* ce plaît à respirer
　　A des charmes trop forts pour n'y pas attirer :
[2] *Othon* 1 1 69—70.
　　Tout m'en plaît, tout m'en charme, et mes premiers scrupules
　　Près d'un si *cher objet* passent pour ridicules.
[3] *Attila* 4 IV 1347—48.
　　Pour un si *cher objet* que je mets en vos bras,
　　Est-ce un prix excessif qu'un si juste trépas ?

pressionist point of view, is surely as happy a description, as could have been found. But in reality only four of the heroines are spoken of as furies.

Émilie is the first of the category. On hearing of the conspiracy which is being formed against him, Augustus, though at the time unconscions of the part which Émilie is playing in it, exclaims:

> Nommez *ce cher objet*, grand Prince, et c'est assez.
> O trahison conçue au sein d'une *furie!*
>
> *Cinna* 4 I 1097.

The next fury in order is the Pulchérie of *Heraclius*, of whom the emperor Phocas says:

> Cette ingrate *furie*, après tant de mépris
> Conspire encor la perte et du père et du fils;
>
> *Héraclius* 1 III 267—68.

Sophonisbe is the third *furie* and traces her claim to the title back to Livy **XXX**. 13, where Syphax describes her as «illam furiam pestemque». In the tragedy of Corneille, Syphax says to Lelius:

> Vous trouverez, Seigneur, cette même *furie*
> Qui seule m'a perdu pour l'avoir trop chérie
>
> *Sophonisbe* 4 II 1213—14.

The fourth and last of the series is the sister of the Emperor Valentinian, of whom Attila says:

> Non, je ne puis plus voir cette ingrate Honorie
> Qu'avec la même horreur qu'on voit une *furie*
>
> *Attila* 5 IV 1641—42.

We therefore see that only four of Corneille's heroines figure under the title which Sainte Beuve has given to the whole class; and that furthermore, the expression *adorable furie* does not occur at all. The nearest approach to it is Cinna's characterization of Émilie as an *«aimable inhumaine»* (*Cinna* 3 III 905) in which far-fetched combination we seem to hear a feeble echo of Castro's Jimena, crying to Rodrigo:

Ay enemigo adorado
Las *Mocedades del Cid* Jornada II escena 6.

The current popular expression of *adorable furie* was, therefore, the coinage of Balzac's neighbor out of his own enthusiasm for Émilie.

---

7. Conclusion.

We have arrived at the end of our investigation. Are we still in doubt as to the reason why the tragic heroines of the great Corneille have gone into oblivion? Or have the foregoing pages perhaps given us a hint as to the cause of their decadence? We have explained the conditions under which the literary masterpieces of French literature came into existence in the seventeenth century. We have demonstrated the faith which the illustrious French authors had in the so-called rules. The present study has further demonstrated the faith which Corneille had in the efficacy of rules, as applied to the creation of heroines. His were heroines according to rule, and this is why they impress us in their ensemble not so much as human beings with human impulses, as automatic figures, who act according to the limitations of their mechanism. We found that Corneille had a certain ideal. He conceived his heroines as political Amazons, thirsting for revenge for wrongs suffered; at the same time we find them endowed with the ideals, the emotions, the wit and the beauty of the great ladies of the seventeenth century. They bewilder and perplex us. They have their haughty moments, their pathetic moments, their comedy moments, their moments of prudery and coquetry and all irrespective of age, nationality or general character. We can understand the tears of Chimène mourning over the death of her father. We are not touched by the tears of Arsinoé, grieving over a political fiasco. We approve of the *politesse* and *esprit* of the comédiennes of the tragedy of Agésilas, where we would gladly pardon abruptness on the part of a young girl like Chimène, hastening to the side of her dying father. We can readily believe in the *beaux yeux* of the idyllic Adromède and the pensive Psyche, but we find it difficult to picture to ourselves the *dangéreux charmes* of the *adorable* Pulchérie already more than fifty years of age, as Corneille expressly tells us. As Pulchérie is the only heroine, whose age Corneille gives in figures, she possesses a unique interest on this account, but at the same time, she arouses our curiosity, if it has not been aroused before, as to the age in general of Corneille's heroines. This point is a delicate one and is veiled in mystery. Voltaire did not hesitate in his maliciousness to challenge Rodogune on this score. This heroine of Corneille's favorite work makes her first appearance with the evil forebodings of a Chimène, Émilie, Pauline, and Laodice, and says timidly to her confidant:

Je ne sais quel malheur aujourd'hui me menace.
Rodogune, 1 V. 299.

On hearing the mention of her lover's name, she entreats her confidant:

Garde-toi de nommer mon vainqueur.
Ma rougeur trahirait les secrets de mon coeur.
Rodogune 1 V. 385-86.

In his commentaries on this scene, Voltaire says: «Remarquez, que tous les discours de Rodogune sont dans le caractère d'une jeune personne qui craint de s'avouer à elle-même les sentiments tendres et honnêtes dont son cœur est touché. Cependant Rodogune n'est point jeune; elle épousa Nicanor, lorsque les deux frères étaient en bas âge; ils ont au moins vingt ans. Cette rougeur, cette timidité, cette innocence, semblent donc un peu outrées pour son âge; elles s'accordent peu avec tant de maximes de politique; elles conviennent encore moins à une femme, qui bientôt demandera la tête de sa belle-mère aux enfants de cette belle-mère».

The same incongruities occur in the character of Viriate. This heroine, as we have already pointed out, is a queen, who on her own declaration does not even know what love is. She aspires to a political marriage with Sertorius. She is concerned only for the welfare of her realm. In the last act too, as we have shown, she seeks glorious revenge on Perpenna, agreeing to marry him so as to have free access to pierce him to the heart. Such is the general character of Viriate. Nevertheless, in her first scene with her confidant, we find the same modesty and timidity as in Rodogune. She hesitates to mention the name of the old Sertorius. She speaks of him as «*un autre choix*» and «*ce héros si cher ; tu le connois Thamire*». Voltaire objects to this element in the character of Viriate. He says: «Cet embarras, cette crainte de nommer celui qu'elle aime, pourraient convenir à une jeune personne timide, et semblent peu faite pour une femme politique».

Hémon, in his notes on Rodogune, takes offense at Voltaire for cavilling over the age of Rodogune, and in justice to Corneille it should be said that he did his best to make the relations of Rodogune and her two lovers plausible. Nevertheless, the spectator cannot but be left in doubt as to her age, as well as to that of other heroines. Corneille does not inform us on this point. We simply know that he manipulated the dates and facts of history to suit his ideas of propriety. We are not allowed to inquire too sharply concerning the age of his captive princesses. Still we cannot refrain from comparing the ages of a few of his heroines. Without citing his authority, Körting[1] tells us that Chimène was only fourteen years old. If this be so, then a young Spanish girl of fourteen served as model to a long line of heroines, who according to history,

---

[1] Körting. Der französische Roman im 17. Jahrhundert. p. 30.

at least, were of widely varying age. In the case of Émilie, Chimène's immediate successor in her method of solving her problem, we know that her father was proscribed by Augustus, twenty years before the opening of the play. Émilie must, therefore, be between twenty and thirty. The Cléopatre of Rodogune, who likewise demands the head of her enmy, is represented as having two sons already grown up to manhood. But an inquiry into the age of Corneille's heroines does not furnish us with satisfactory results. We are therefore compelled to accept our heroines as being of an ideal age. In the time of Corneille, it is not probable that many of the spectators troubled themselves over this point. Realism had not yet made its appearance upon the stage. No actress had yet been found who for the sake of realism would have voluntarily disguised or disfigured her own charms. It is, therefore, safe to assume that the actresses of Corneille's time in their sumptuous seventeenth century toilettes, took good care not to look any older than possible, and that they felt quite justified in vying in personal attractiveness with the great ladies of the epoch. They were heroines of ideal age.

In taking leave of the heroines of Corneille, we cannot but acknowledge that in spite of their monotony from the point of view of the present day, they have not been entirely without interest. They have revived many memories of ancient and mediaeval history, as well as of the century in which they ruled the stage. Many of them too in themselves have stirred us by their eloquence, and have compelled our respect by their unflinching adherence to their duty. Why, then, have they not been able to hold their own among the dramatic heroines of the world's literature? We would offer two theories. First, Corneille was not a psychologist, and he, therefore, could not create heroines who should be real human beings from a psychological standpoint. He did not have a deep insight into the human heart, and the feminine heart was a sealed book to him. With his own cool deliberation and self-consciousness he created his heroines mechanically and idealized them according to his own heroic ideals.

The second cause of the fate of Corneille's heroines lies in the fact that the poet was specifically a man of his century. What he might have been, had he lived in the nineteenth century, we do not know. But as father of the French tragedy, he represents to us now the most illustrious ancestor of a literary genus which has become extinct. The classic French tragedy ruled the world for two centuries. It is now a thing of the past. Founded on a set of imaginary but none the less arbitary rules, it became crystallized into the hard and uninteresting form which we find in the inferior plays of Corneille and of the host of minor poets of different nations who continued the school which was brought to perfection by him. The heroines of Corneille illustrate by themselves the danger of applying rules to the creation of human beings; as Mercier very truly said, the rules «mutilated the characters». It does not suffice to pattern one heroine after her predecessor, however successful this predecessor may have been. It is not enough to devise one or two situations and a series of conventional attributes, and make them do service for forty years. Finally it is not true that the language of a Malherbe or a Boileau is the only language which a dramatic poet may venture to use. A dramatic genius will always use the language of a genius, and it will live after him, without becoming petrified and lifeless. But this was not the opinion in the seventeenth century. The classic French drama had its own *stil noble*, and if we examine the language of the French poet-dramatists from Mairet to Voltaire, we shall gradually perceive that it becomes reduced to a series of conventional formulas.[1] Look through the quo-

---

[1] Kinne. Formulas in the Language of the French Poet-Dramatists of the Seventeenth Century. Strassburg Dissertation. Boston 1891.

tations so profusely scattered through the present essay, and you will recognize many of these formulas and note the monotonous effect which they produce in the delineation of the heroines. The tragic heroines of Corneille were created according to a system. This system was their doom. Still we are grateful to the great Corneille for the creation of several of his most famous heroines. Chimène, Émilie and Pauline, through their nobility of character, their «grandeur d'âme» will always live. They are already immortal in the hearts of the French people.

VITA.

I was born in Boston, Mass. U. S. A. November 5th. 1866. My early education was received in the Boston public schools. In 1885 I graduated from the Boston Latin School; and in 1889 from Harvard University with the degree of A. B. In 1890, I entered the University of Leipzig, where I remained for three semesters. Returning temporarily to America, I occupied the position of instructor in Romance Languages in Western Reserve University, Cleveland, Ohio, where I remained for three semesters, returning in the summer of 1894 to Europe. In October of that year, I entered the University of Strassburg, for the purpose of continuing my studies under Professor Gröber. For the many valuable hours of instruction which I have spent in the lecture-rooms and seminars of the above-mentioned German universities, I would take this opportunity of expressing my thanks to the following professors and docents: in Leipzig, — Biedermann, Elster, Flügel, Masius, Springer, Strümpell, Wülcker, Wundt and Zarncke; in Strassburg, — Brandl, Gröber, Hübschmann, Koeppel, Martin, Miller, Röhrig and Schneegans.

CHARLES CARLTON AYER.

www.ingramcontent.com/pod-product-compliance
Lightning Source LLC
Chambersburg PA
CBHW030347170426
43202CB00010B/1280